# OPEN
# SANDWICHES

# Trine Hahnemann

# OPEN SANDWICHES

## 70 smørrebrød ideas for morning, noon and night

Photography by Columbus Leth

*Hardie Grant*

QUADRILLE

**Publishing Director** Sarah Lavelle
**Commissioning Editor** Céline Hughes
**Creative Director** Helen Lewis
**Senior Designer** Katherine Keeble
**Photographer** Columbus Leth
**Production Director** Vincent Smith
**Production Controller** Nikolaus Ginelli

First published in 2018 by Quadrille, an imprint of Hardie Grant Publishing
Quadrille, 52–54 Southwark Street, London SE1 1UN
quadrille.com

Cataloguing-In-Publication Data: A catalogue record for this book
is available from the British Library.

Reprinted in 2019
10 9 8 7 6 5 4 3 2

ISBN 978 178713 125 5

Printed in China

# Foreword

*Smørrebrød*, or open sandwiches, are easy, healthy, everyday food. They are ingrained in the daily Danish food culture starting from an early age. When we move from baby food to solids, one of the first things we try is tiny squares of rye bread with butter and cheese, or liver pâté, or, like my children, hummus. Eating rye bread with toppings is for Danes as rice is for the people of Japan.

All Danes have a favourite *smørrebrød*. They can be elaborate constructions, but when they are everyday eating we call them *madder* instead. My favourite in summertime is potato, or salami with potato and crispy onions (see page 24). In winter, roast beef. If I am in a hurry and more-or-less eating lunch standing, it will often be a piece of cheese, or avocado, or if I have a craving for something sweet, then fig spread (see page 43) or banana.

When I was a little girl and spent the summer at my grandparents' beach house, my *morfar* (grandfather) would always make me three pieces of *smørrebrød*. I would go into the sea and have my last swim of the day. *Morfar* would be waiting with my bath robe and my three *madder*. There would be two savouries, which varied depending on the kitchen leftovers, such as potatoes and meatballs; the third would always be with raisins. Eating my supper, sitting on the beach, feeling the day coming to an end with my *morfar* at my side, will always be a very fond memory. My love for *madder* might be hidden right there.

I am really proud to share these ideas, and my sincere hope is that these recipes will inspire you to get on board with a truly unique Danish tradition that is such a big part of my life.

# History and tradition

*Smørrebrød* (pronounced smuhr-broht) means, in Danish, simply 'butter on bread'. But it means so much more than that: it is, without doubt, a food culture unique to Denmark, indeed, one of Denmark's contributions to the world of food.

It is something that most Danes have grown up with and eaten daily, either as the simple kind we call *madder*, or in a more elaborate form as *smørrebrød*. It is the traditional Danish lunch, and it dates back to at least the Middle Ages. Initially, the rye bread, spread with butter or fat, would have various leftovers served on top, but that has grown over time into its own genre of food.

The whole concept of *smørrebrød* really evolved as fresh ingredients became more readily available. In the 19th century, fresh fish and meat started to be sold at small markets, and little local factories started popping up to make *pålæg*: the name for all the things we use to top the rye bread, such as cold cuts, cheese, vegetables and fruit.

In 1880, the elaborate *smørrebrød* was developed, with a multitude of different toppings and combinations. A whole new food culture took form, with its own rules. In fact, a whole new system of education was established, dedicated to learning the art of *smørrebrød*. It was designed for women; after graduation you could call yourself *smørrebrødsjomfru*, which means an open-faced-sandwich virgin!

The famous Danish writer Hans Christian Andersen is known for his love of food, including *smørrebrød*. When he paid visits to bourgeois families in Copenhagen during the mid 19th century, he was sometimes disappointed about the supper he was offered. Anticipating this, he would eat *smørrebrød* before leaving home, or order some from his housekeeper for when he returned. He wrote in his diary that it was to settle his nerves.

*Smørrebrød* also became the first Danish takeaway. In Copenhagen and larger cities, *smørrebrød* shops began to open at the turn of the 19th century. It became very common to go to those and pick up *smørrebrød* for dinner, when you wanted a treat yourself, or to entertain guests. The takeaway places still exist.

Dance halls would also serve *smørrebrød*. It was very popular for supper because it was quick to eat, which meant young people had more time for dancing, instead of having to spend the evening tied to a dinner table.

There are also restaurants specializing in *smørrebrød*, including one family restaurant that opened in 1880. They offer their customers a menu of *smørrebrøds-seddel*, listing the options available. Denmark's oldest restaurant, Lumskebugten, serves *smørrebrød* for lunch every day, and it is my favourite place for it in Copenhagen. It's classic, the produce is great, and it's made with respect and love. I wish the walls could talk and tell stories from past times.

*Smørrebrød* is gaining in popularity after some years of dwindling interest during the last years of the 20th century. There were various reasons for the downturn. One reason was that all the toppings and rye bread became mass produced, so the quality deteriorated, becoming more salty and sweet, but also more bland. Another was the impact of competition from shawarma, burger joints and other fast-food concepts.

But things are looking up. The new focus is on super-modern, simple *smørrebrød*, with home-baked, high-quality rye bread back at the centre. Everything must be home-made. Artisan schnapps, and beer from microbreweries, are part of the concept again. Schnapps is often served ice cold, always poured to the rim of the mini wine glass in which it comes. In *smørrebrød* restaurants, these glasses are kept in the freezer. When drinking schnapps, you will get a burning sensation, as it is usual to down the glass in one. For women, it's okay to drink it in two; we call this 'to bite it over'. In the cold, dark Scandinavian winter months, back in the good old days, it was drunk to warm you up and also believed to be good for the circulation. That could be just an excuse, though...

At the table, before you start eating, there is always a toast with the first glass of schnapps. You raise the glass, taking care that not a single drop is spilled, toast, then drink, throwing your head back. Then you raise your empty glass again. *Skål*. Feel free to do the same but, I warn you, be careful: it can be dangerous to drink too many.

The legacy of *smørrebrød* is here to stay. I am so proud – genuinely pleased – that the interest in *smørrebrød* grows steadily and the culture is expanding. I think telling the story of your roots through food is important. I carry so many memories with me, most of them connected to meals: what we ate, how that food was made and where it came from. I am thrilled to share

my traditions with the world. I do hope the story of *smørrebrød* will spread ever further and that more people will enjoy a piece of unique Danish gastronomy on super-healthy, tasty rye bread.

# The unwritten rules

Must food cultures have rules, and they are often unwritten. You learn about them when growing up, but not by being told; it is more subtle, like a kind of unconscious osmosis. I will try to explain them here, as I learned them from my family. (There may be unwritten rules in other families or other regions of which I am not aware.)

Let's start with the bread: primarily it should be rye bread, with a few exceptions. It should be cut in relatively thin slices.

Then there is the butter: it *has* to be salted. However, I have adjusted this rule over the years and, unlike those of my *mormor*'s (grandmother's) generation, I do not always need butter. My rule is that there has to be butter if the topping would otherwise soak the bread, or if it is important for the flavour. If your topping is sweet, such as prawns, fig spread, chocolate or raisins, then you will need salty butter to balance it out. However, the question of butter or no butter is personal, and I know a lot of people will disagree with me!

Next, there must be a main topping as well as a combination of condiments to add. A specific combination must have at least three of the following flavour components: salt, sweet, sour, bitter, and umami. In terms of texture, there should be something soft and something crunchy. If the topping is a fatty meat, you will need a light, sweet-and-sour condiment. If the meat is lean, there should be a rich or creamy sauce. In other words, in both flavour and texture, you want balance.

*Smørrebrød* must look appetizing. There should be more than one colour, as well as herbs to garnish. Cress is the most common garnish. I grow my own, which is easy on your windowsill: place the seeds on damp cotton wool and they will grow in 3–5 days.

As in all food, there are trends in *smørrebrød*. Thirty years ago, it came with little bread, too much topping, and lots of non-edible decoration. Now it's different. The bread is very important – in fact the main ingredient – and everything on it is part of what you eat.

If this is sounding complicated, don't worry – it really isn't. See it like this super-simple version:

bread **+** butter

*then* hard-boiled eggs (soft and fatty)
**+** tomatoes (firm and sweet-tart)
**+** creamy mayonnaise

*finally,* salt **+** pepper **+** cress

That's it! You've got a classic piece of *smørrebrød*. Do elaborate on the combinations; there's no reward for being boring, and interesting toppings are always welcome. Also, as you sit at the *smorgasbord* when everybody is composing their own *smørrebrød*, it pays to observe and spot ideas for interesting combinations.

Finally, you must eat *smørrebrød* in the correct order:

**1** Always herring first.
**2** Then salmon or other fish.
**3** Then meat or vegetables.
**4** Cheese always comes at the end.

Danes do enjoy inviting foreigners over for a *smørrebrød* lunch, not letting them in on the unwritten rules, then laughing before they help them out. It's not cruel, just Danish humour!

Still, there are things which are just not done: combining herring and meat on an open sandwich, or any fish and meat for that matter, except maybe bacon; salmon is never accompanied by rémoulade or mayo; roasted onion is never eaten with smoked fish; the only pickle you can have with fish must be mixed into rémoulade... I could go on, and there's much more.

On the other hand, what are rules if we do not test them? See what works for your palate. Good luck and *velbekomme*.

# Everyday

Everyday open sandwiches are called *madder* in Denmark. We eat them casually out of our lunch boxes or in the evening, when we don't want to cook a warm supper; a quick bite if we don't have time for more. When my children were small, on those nights when I had no intention of cooking, we would have *madder*. I would slice rye bread, boil eggs, find some leftovers, then dig some tomatoes and cucumber out of the fridge and fetch bananas from the fruit bowl. I would prepare the toppings, then arrange them nicely on boards and serving dishes. We would all sit around the big kitchen table and assemble the *madder* of our choice.

As a child, I loved this kind of eating in our small kitchen, just my mother and me, usually on those evenings after my grandfather had mailed us a really good salami from his local butcher on the island of Ærø. My parents had very little money, so eating salami *madder* was special. I still remember how it tasted in our kitchen in Copenhagen.

The seasons play a pivotal role in the toppings for *madder*. Potato, tomato and prawns are for summer, while meat and pickles feature heavily during autumn and winter. No matter what the season, though, good rye bread is vital both for texture and taste. It has to be the very dense, dark sourdough type. I always have a home-made rye bread (see page 138) in my kitchen.

However, there are certain toppings that traditionally come on white bread. When I was growing up, white bread was a treat, and the adults would say, "If you eat your rye bread, you can have white bread." So, after my three pieces of rye, if I was still hungry, I was allowed a piece of white bread with butter and a thin layer of chocolate on top.

# Tomato, egg and mayonnaise

You can use cottage cheese instead of mayonnaise here, if you prefer. Or change the herbs: chopped chives, chervil and dill will work well instead of cress. *Serves 4*

> 4 slices of rye bread
> salted butter
> 2 large tomatoes
> 2 hard-boiled eggs (see page 145)
> 2 tbsp Classic mayonnaise (see page 146)
> 2 tbsp cress
> sea salt flakes and freshly ground black pepper

Place the rye bread slices on a work top and spread the butter evenly on each slice. Slice the tomatoes. Cut each egg into 4 slices, and place 2 slices of egg with 1 slice of tomato in the middle on each bread.

Divide the mayonnaise between the open sandwiches, place the cress on top and sprinkle with salt and pepper.

**Right:**
Bringing your own open sandwiches into work in a box became commonplace with industrialization. Before that, farmers would take bread, butter and leftovers out into the fields.

# Pork, onion and asier

Use turkey or chicken breast instead of pork, or indeed any
leftover meat. If you don't have asier, you can use Sweet and sour
cucumber or Pickled gherkins (see pages 163 and 162). *Serves 4*

   1 small onion
   2 tbsp lemon juice
   1 tsp sea salt flakes
   2 tsp caster (granulated) sugar
   4 slices of rye bread
   salted butter
   4 slices of roast pork
   4 slices of Asier (see page 160)
   4–6 pieces of pork crackling

Cut the onion into wedges and place them in a bowl with the
lemon juice, salt and sugar. Leave for 2–3 hours, then drain.

   Place the rye bread slices on a work top and spread the butter
evenly on each slice. Place 1 slice of roast pork on each bread
and divide the onions between them, together with a slice of
asier. Cut or crush the crackling and sprinkle on top.

# Avocado and cottage cheese

Instead of cress and chive flowers, try chopped parsley leaves, chives or coriander. *Serves 4*

> 4 slices of rye bread
> 2 avocados
> 2 tbsp lemon juice
> 4 tbsp cottage cheese
> 2 tbsp cress
> some chive flowers (optional)
> 1 tsp Aleppo pepper
> sea salt flakes

Place the rye bread slices on a work top. Halve the avocados, remove the stones, peel, then cut them into slices. Place the avocado slices on the rye bread (you don't need butter with this creamy topping), sprinkle with lemon juice, then add 1 tbsp cottage cheese to each. Sprinkle with cress and chive flowers (if using), then with Aleppo pepper and salt.

# Egg salad

This is a classic in many countries. I don't much like the ready-made stuff and never buy it, but I do love a freshly made egg salad. It must be made from organic eggs and contain a lot of herbs and a bit of lemon juice, so it feels fresh. Instead of cress, you can use chopped chives. *Serves 4*

4 hard-boiled eggs (see page 145)
½ celery stick, finely chopped
4 tbsp chopped dill
3 tbsp Classic mayonnaise (see page 146)
1–2 tbsp lemon juice
2 tbsp full-fat natural yogurt
sea salt flakes and freshly ground black pepper
2 tomatoes
4 slices of rye bread
4 tbsp cress

Chop the eggs finely and place them in a mixing bowl. Add the celery, dill, Classic mayonnaise, lemon juice and yogurt. Mix gently and season to taste with salt and pepper.

Cut the tomatoes into halves, scrape out the seeds, then cut the flesh into thin slices.

Place the rye bread slices on a cutting board, divide the egg salad between them and decorate with tomato slices and the cress, sprinkling with more pepper.

# Potatoes — 4 ways

This is an absolute Danish classic, and some people not familiar with the *smørrebrød* tradition find it a bit odd… that only lasts until they have tasted it. As with many of the other *smørrebrød* recipes, these are made from leftovers. In a Danish household, the leftover potatoes from dinner are often saved for the next day and used to make a *kartoffelmad. All recipes serve 4*

## Aubergine mayonnaise and bacon

4 slices of rye bread
salted butter
1–2 slices of bacon, cut into lardons
4–6 cold, boiled new potatoes
8 tsp Aubergine mayonnaise
    (see page 148)
small handful of chervil leaves,
    or parsley, dill, or chives
freshly ground black pepper

Place the rye bread slices on a work top and spread the butter evenly on each slice.

Fry the bacon in a dry frying pan in its own fat until crisp and light brown.

Slice the potatoes and place them on the rye bread. Place 2 tsp Aubergine mayonnaise on each in a rough line, or pipe a long strip on top if you're feeling fancy.

Divide the bacon between the slices, decorate with the chervil and sprinkle with pepper.

## Mayonnaise and double onions

4 slices of rye bread
salted butter
4–6 cold, boiled new potatoes
8 tsp Classic mayonnaise
    (see page 146)
2 tbsp finely chopped red onion
4 tbsp Crispy onions (see page 156)
4 tbsp cress
sea salt flakes and freshly ground
    black pepper

Place the rye bread slices on a work top and spread the butter evenly on each slice. Slice the potatoes and place them on the bread.

Place 2 tsp Classic mayonnaise on each in a rough line, or pipe a long strip on top if you're feeling fancy. On one side of the mayonnaise place the red onion, and on the other the Crispy onions and cress. Sprinkle it all with salt and pepper.

# Tarragon mayonnaise and capers

4 slices of rye bread
salted butter
2 tbsp capers, drained and rinsed
1 tsp olive oil
4–6 cold, boiled new potatoes
8 tsp Tarragon mayonnaise
    (see page 148)
small handful of celery leaves
small handful of tarragon leaves
freshly ground black pepper

Place the rye bread slices on a work top and spread the butter evenly on each slice. Fry the capers in the olive oil in a small frying pan, until crisp. Place them on a piece of kitchen paper to blot off excess fat.

Slice the potatoes and place them on the rye bread. Place 2 tsp Tarragon mayonnaise on each in a rough line, or pipe a long strip on top if you're feeling fancy.

Place the fried capers on one side of the mayonnaise. Decorate with celery and tarragon leaves and sprinkle with pepper.

# Leek and lemon

1 small leek
200ml (¾ cup) flavourless oil
4 slices of rye bread
salted butter
4–6 cold, boiled new potatoes
2 tbsp Pesto (see page 156)
4 tbsp capers, drained and rinsed
zest of about ½ unwaxed lemon,
    cut into julienne
freshly ground black pepper

Cut the leek into thin slices on an angle, rinse them in cold water and then dry them well. Fry the slices in the oil in a big frying pan until crisp. Let them rest on a piece of kitchen paper, to blot off excess fat.

Place the rye bread slices on a work top and spread the butter evenly on each slice. Slice the potatoes and place them on the rye bread. Divide the Pesto evenly over the potatoes, then top with capers.

Decorate with the fried leeks and the lemon zest, then sprinkle with pepper.

# Salami

If you ask Danes which casual, everyday *smørrebrød* they would eat, many would mention *spegepølse*, a smoked, dry-cured salami. Here are three ways of eating salami on rye bread.
*Serves 6*

> 6 slices of rye bread
> salted butter
> 18 slices of salami
> 2 cold, boiled potatoes, sliced
> 4 tbsp Crispy onions (see page 156)
> 4 tbsp Rémoulade (see page 164)
> 2 tbsp cress, plus more to decorate
> 2 tsp Pesto (see page 156)
> 1 spring onion (scallion), finely chopped

Place the rye bread slices on a cutting board and spread the butter evenly on each slice. Place 3 slices of salami on each.

Top 2 sandwiches with slices of potatoes and 1 tbsp Crispy onions on each.

For the next 2, divide the Rémoulade, cress and 1 tbsp Crispy onions on top of each.

For the last 2, top with Pesto and spring onion. Decorate with a bit of cress.

# Tomato, aubergine mayonnaise and Parma ham

There are seemingly endless combinations of tomatoes and rye bread. When I was a young girl, we would mostly eat tomatoes in the summer. That has changed, and tomatoes are now available all year round, but they are still tastier in the summer. *Serves 4*

4 slices of Parma or Serrano ham
4 slices of rye bread
4 medium tomatoes
8 tsp Aubergine mayonnaise (see page 148)
4 tbsp watercress
freshly ground black pepper

Preheat the oven to fan 200°C/425°F/gas 7. Place the ham slices on a baking sheet lined with baking parchment, and cook for about 8 minutes. Take out of the oven and leave to cool, then crumble them with your fingers.

Place the rye bread slices on a work top. Slice the tomatoes and place them on the bread, then place 2 tsp Aubergine mayonnaise on each.

Divide the crumbled ham on top, decorate with the watercress and sprinkle with pepper.

# Rullepølse and cornichons

You can find the recipe for *rullepølse* in the Basics chapter, and of course it makes more than you need for 4 sandwiches. I make it, then cut it up into smaller pieces and freeze it. It takes a bit of time to do, but it is not difficult and it is really tasty. *Serves 4*

4 slices of rye bread
salted butter
8 slices of Rullepølse (see page 171)
4 tsp Dijon mustard
8 cornichons
4 tbsp capers
1 small red onion, thinly sliced
4 tbsp chopped dill
freshly ground black pepper

**Variation:**
Use Asier or Pickled gherkins (see pages 160 and 162) instead of cornichons, and parsley instead of dill. These can also be served with Pesto (see page 156).

Place the rye bread slices on a work top and spread the butter evenly on each slice.

Place 2 slices of Rullepølse on each slice of bread. Then spread 1 tsp of Dijon mustard on each open sandwich, and top with cornichons, capers, onion slices and dill. Sprinkle with pepper.

# Russian salad on rye

Another great vegetarian classic. There are endless variations on Russian salad recipes, but here is mine, which contains freshly grated raw beetroot instead of boiled cubes. It's sweet, fresh and spicy, and goes really well with rye bread. *Serves 4*

1 sour apple
1 celery stick
50g (1¾oz) beetroot, coarsely grated
4 tbsp full-fat crème fraîche
2 tbsp horseradish, grated
4 tbsp lime juice
sea salt flakes and freshly ground black pepper
4 slices of rye bread
salted butter
4 tbsp cress

Chop the apple and celery into small cubes and put them in a mixing bowl, then add the beetroot. Fold in the crème fraîche, horseradish and lime juice, then season to taste with some salt and pepper.

Place the rye bread slices on a work top and spread the butter evenly on each slice. Place 2 tbsp of the Russian salad on each rye bread, then decorate with cress and sprinkle with pepper.

# Baked celeriac

Essentially a useful recipe for leftovers, this can of course also be made from scratch (as below). I make *smørrebrød* like this when I have leftover vegetables like celeriac, beetroot, cauliflower, or carrot available. Many of my *smørrebrød* recipes come from figuring out how I can use up dinner leftovers the next day, served on rye bread. *Serves 4*

½ celeriac root (celery root)
1 tbsp olive oil
1 tbsp sea salt flakes
freshly ground black pepper
50g (⅓ cup) hazelnuts, chopped
50g (3½ tbsp) salted butter, plus more for the bread
leaves from 1 tarragon sprig
4 slices of rye bread
4 tbsp cress

Preheat the oven to fan 200°C/425°F/gas 7.

Scrub the celeriac in water, cut off any dirty peel, place it on a baking sheet with the cut surface downwards, brush with olive oil and sprinkle with the salt and some pepper. Bake it for 1 hour. Take it out and keep warm.

Toast the hazelnuts lightly in a dry frying pan, then add the butter and tarragon. Let it cook until the butter is brown, then remove from the heat.

Place the rye bread slices on a work top and spread the butter evenly on each slice. Cut the celeriac into 12 slices. Place them on the rye bread slices and, with a spoon, spread the brown-roasted hazelnuts over, then decorate with the cress and sprinkle with pepper. Serve right away.

# Pork rillettes

For me, this is real winter food, just right for when one needs
a meal with more heft. I eat the rillettes for lunch with pickles;
I do enjoy eating the same thing for a few days in a row. I find
that it's like a small celebration of one's food, before you move
on to something else. This also makes a great starter. *Serves 4*

**for the rillettes**
750g (1lb 10oz) pork belly
750g (1lb 10oz) pork shoulder
   or neck
2 bay leaves
4 sprigs of thyme
1 onion, stuck with 4 cloves
5 juniper berries

sea salt flakes and freshly ground
   black pepper

**for the smørrebrød**
4 slices of rye bread
200g (7oz) rillettes
2 Pickled gherkins (see page 162)
dill sprigs

For the rillettes: skin and bone the meat, but leave the fat on;
it's important for the quality of the rillettes. Cut the meat
into batons about 3 x 1 x 1cm (1¼ x ⅜ x ⅜in). Place in a heavy
saucepan for which you have a tight-fitting lid. Slowly heat until
the fat starts to melt, stirring all the time. Add the remaining
ingredients and cover with the lid. Let simmer over a very low
heat for 5 hours, until it is very soft and tender. It is important
that the meat doesn't roast, but just simmers in the fat.

Lift the meat from the saucepan into a bowl. Pour the fat
through a sieve into a second bowl and set aside, discarding all
the flavourings. Tear the meat into fine shreds with a couple of
forks. Season to taste with salt and pepper and pack it tightly
into glasses, which you have sterilized by filling with boiling
water, or a terrine. Heat the fat in a pan until liquid, then pour
it over the rillettes until the surface is covered, to seal the pork.
Leave to cool, cover with cling film or baking parchment, then
refrigerate until the fat has set. It keeps for weeks in the fridge.

Before serving, remove the fat from the top. Place the rye
bread slices on a work top and spread a layer of rillettes on each.
Slice the gherkins and place them on top. Sprinkle with salt and
pepper and decorate with dill sprigs.

# Liver pâté

This is a classic that can be served plain on less elaborate everyday *smørrebrød*, or gussied up and served warm with a lot of bacon and mushrooms. The recipe for the liver pâté is from my grandmother; I have never tried another I thought was better. *Serves 4*

10 mushrooms
50g (1¾oz) bacon lardons
8 slices of rye bread
200g (7oz) Liver pâté (see page 153)
2 cold, boiled potatoes, sliced
2 tbsp Crispy onions (see page 156)
2 Pickled beetroot (see page 162)
2 tsp cress
8 slices of cucumber
freshly ground black pepper

Trim the mushrooms, quarter them and fry together with the bacon in a frying pan.

Place the slices of rye bread on a work top and spread Liver pâté on each slice. Now top 2 pieces with fried bacon and mushrooms. Top another 2 pieces with slices of potatoes and Crispy onions. Top the next 2 with Pickled beetroot and cress. At last – the simplest one – place slices of fresh cucumber on top of the liver pâté on the last 2 slices. Sprinkle them all with some pepper.

# Fish cakes

We call these *fiskefrikadeller* and they are like meatballs, just made with fish! The name *frikadeller* comes from the Italian *fritta*, so it means anything small and round that is fried: meat, fish, or vegetable. We mostly eat these with Rémoulade and Sweet and sour cucumber salad. *Serves 4*

### for the fish cakes

500g (1lb 2oz) cod fillet, or other
    white fish fillet
1 small onion, finely grated
2 tbsp capers, rinsed and drained,
    chopped
2 eggs, lightly beaten
3½ tbsp double (heavy) cream
2–3 tbsp plain (all-purpose) flour
1 tbsp finely chopped tarragon leaves
2 tbsp finely chopped dill
sea salt flakes and freshly ground
    black pepper
a little salted butter and olive oil

### for the smørrebrød

4 slices of rye bread
salted butter
8 fish cakes
4 tbsp Rémoulade (see page 164)
4 tbsp Sweet and sour cucumber
    (see page 163)
4 tsp capers, rinsed and drained
4 small dill sprigs

Chop the cod finely in a food processor (make sure there are no bones). Add all the other ingredients except the butter and oil and mix well, seasoning with salt and pepper.

Heat the oil and butter in a frying pan. Form the mixture into small oval balls with a spoon and fry them for 4–6 minutes on each side.

Place the rye bread slices on a work top and spread the butter evenly on each slice. Place 2 of the fish cakes on each piece of rye bread.

Spoon Rémoulade down the middle of each slice, then Sweet and sour cucumber alongside, then sprinkle with capers and pepper, adding a dill sprig on top.

# Banana, strawberry, raspberry and chocolate

I know this will be a surprise for many people: *smørrebrød* with sweet and very simple toppings; rye bread with banana is very common. Less surprisingly, they are most children's favourites. However, my very grown-up husband often eats them, and still with great joy. He especially enjoys *pålægschokolade* (chocolate topping) if it is homemade, though it can be bought everywhere in Denmark, in dark and milk chocolate varieties. Here, the butter is even more important than usual, because it binds together the topping and the rye bread. *Serves 2–4*

> 8 slices of rye bread
> salted butter
> 100g (1 cup) strawberries
> 2 bananas
> 100g (¾ cup) raspberries
> Paper-thin chocolate pieces (see page 154)

Place the rye bread slices on a work top and spread the butter evenly on each slice.

Rinse and hull the strawberries and cut each in half or in quarters. Slice the bananas. Divide the strawberries, bananas, raspberries and chocolate pieces between the rye bread slices and serve.

# Dried fig paste, raisins and apple

Another Danish tradition, and a staple of my childhood, is dried fig paste. It has always been one of the things I eat on rye bread. Usually I have raisins in the cupboard, or an apple in the fruit bowl, so these *smørrebrød* are often enjoyed at my house.
*Serves 4*

12 slices of rye bread
salted butter
2 apples
finely grated zest and juice of 1 unwaxed lemon
8 slices of Fig paste (see page 155)
150g (1 cup) raisins

Place the rye bread slices on a work top and spread the butter evenly on each slice.

Core the apples. Cut each into 8 slices and sprinkle with a bit of lemon juice. Place the apple on 4 slices of the rye bread, scattering over the lemon zest. Place 2 slices of Fig paste on 4 more slices of the rye bread. Finally, divide the raisins between the last 4 slices of rye bread.

# Tomato, avocado and cottage cheese

A classic everyday *smørrebrød*, especially good in the summer when the best tomatoes are around. I have eaten this all my life and found references to it in a cookbook from 1949, along with a range of suggestions about how to eat tomatoes on rye bread!
*Serves 4*

4 slices of rye bread
2 tomatoes
2 avocados
4 tbsp cottage cheese
1 tsp finely grated unwaxed lemon zest
1 tbsp cress
sea salt flakes and freshly ground black pepper

Place the rye bread slices on a work top. Slice the tomatoes. Halve the avocados, remove the stones, peel them, then cut them into slices, too.

Place the avocado slices on the buttered bread, then the tomato slices. Spread or dollop on the cottage cheese, then sprinkle lemon zest and cress on the top, along with a smattering of salt and pepper. Serve right away.

**Variation:**
Use Classic mayonnaise (see page 146) instead of cottage cheese.

# Lightly cured pork tenderloin and rhubarb

Rhubarb compote is very versatile, and a great match with pork. Traditionally, pork tenderloin is served with fried, soft brown onions. This is my summer recipe: a bit lighter and with the fresh taste of summer produce from rhubarb. *Serves 4*

### for the brine

50g (¼ cup) coarse sea salt
20g (1½ tbsp) granulated sugar
5 sprigs of thyme
1 bay leaf
1 tsp black peppercorns

### for the pork

1 pork tenderloin
1 tbsp salted butter

### for the smørrebrød

4 slices of rye bread
salted butter
4 butterhead lettuce leaves
8 slices of fried tenderloin
4 tbsp Rhubarb compote (see page 159)
freshly ground black pepper
handful of dill sprigs

Pour 500ml (2 cups) water into a large saucepan, then add all the brine ingredients. Bring to the boil, then reduce the heat and let it simmer until the salt and sugar have dissolved. Leave to cool completely.

Trim the tenderloin of its fat and any silverskin you find. Place it in a bowl or plastic container and pour over the cold brine. Cover and leave in the fridge overnight.

The next day, lift the tenderloin out of the brine and pat it dry with kitchen paper. Heat the butter in a frying pan and fry the tenderloin for about 5 minutes on each side. Let it cool down. Cut it into 8 pieces at an angle.

Place the rye bread slices on a work top and spread the butter evenly on each slice. Place 1 lettuce leaf on each bread slice and then 2 pieces of tenderloin. Place 1 tbsp Rhubarb compote on top of each, then sprinkle with pepper and top with dill sprigs.

**Variation:**
Instead of pork, try this with leftover chicken or beef.

# Cheese — 4 ways

Cheese is often served after a meal, but on *madder* it is eaten at breakfast, lunch and dinner! Any of these are great with tea, beer or wine. *All recipes serve 4*

## Cheddar and rhubarb

> 4 slices of sourdough bread
> salted butter
> 12 slices of cheddar cheese
> 4 tbsp Rhubarb compote
>    (see page 159)
> 4 tsp cress

Place the sourdough bread slices on a work top and spread the butter on each slice.

Top with the slices of cheese, then dollop each with 1 tbsp of the rhubarb. Finally, sprinkle with the cress.

## Sheep's cheese and quince

> 4 slices of rye bread
> salted butter
> 12 slices of hard sheep's cheese
> 12 slices of quince paste
> 1 sprig of wild chervil or dill

Place the rye bread slices on a work top and spread the butter on each slice.

Top with the slices of cheese, then the quince paste slices. Finish with the wild chervil or dill.

## Cream cheese and redcurrant

4 slices of sourdough bread
salted butter
100g (½ cup) cream cheese
4 tbsp Shaken redcurrants
    (see page 159)
4 tsp sorrel, or microherbs, or cress

Place the sourdough bread slices on a work top and spread the butter on each slice.

Evenly spread with the cream cheese, then the redcurrants, and decorate with the sorrel, microherbs or cress.

## Blue cheese and pear

1 pear
2 tsp salted butter
1 tbsp honey
1 vanilla pod, split and seeds
    scraped out
4 slices of rye bread
200g (7oz) Danish blue cheese, sliced

Cut the pear into wedges, leaving the stalk on and core in, if possible (it looks good!). Melt the butter in a frying pan, then fry the pears for a few minutes on each side. Add the honey and vanilla and turn gently. Turn off the heat and leave to cool in the pan.

Toast the rye bread, then top with the blue cheese. Finish with the wedges of pear.

# Eggs – 3 ways

I have eaten countless egg-topped open sandwiches. They're the ones I often end up making, because I always have eggs in the kitchen, they are easy to cook and I have a lot of herbs in my front yard. *Each serves 4*

# Prawns and mayo

4 slices of rye bread
salted butter
4 hard-boiled eggs (see page 145)
4 tsp Classic mayonnaise
    (see page 146)
100g (3½oz) cooked small prawns
4 tsp cress
freshly ground black pepper

Place the rye bread slices on a work top and spread the butter evenly on each slice.

Slice the eggs and place on each slice of rye bread, then place a long strip of mayonnaise down the centre and place the prawns on top. Decorate with cress and sprinkle with black pepper.

# Tomato and pesto

4 slices of rye bread
salted butter
1 tomato
4 hard-boiled eggs (see page 145)
4 tsp Pesto (see page 156)
4 tsp cress
freshly ground black pepper

Place the rye bread slices on a work top and spread the butter evenly on each slice. Halve the tomatoes, scrape out the seeds, then cut into slices.

Cut the eggs into slices and place on each slice of rye bread, then add the Pesto, in a long strip. Lay the tomato slices on top and finally sprinkle with cress and black pepper.

# Cottage cheese and chives

4 slices of rye bread
salted butter
4 tbsp cottage cheese
4 tbsp finely chopped chives
4 hard-boiled eggs (see page 145)
freshly ground black pepper

Place the rye bread slices on a work top and spread the butter evenly on each slice.

Mix the cottage cheese and most of the chives in a small bowl, saving some chives for decoration.

Cut the egg into slices and place on each slice of rye bread, then place the cottage cheese on top, decorated with the reserved chives. Sprinkle with some black pepper.

# Ham, spinach and sunny-side-up egg

This is a *smørrebrød* that is good for breakfast. Instead of ham, you can use bacon. I like to eat something like this on Saturdays or Sundays, when I have time to linger over breakfast, drink coffee, and read the newspaper. *Serves 4*

> 400g (14oz) spinach
> 3 tbsp salted butter, plus more for the bread
> 4 eggs
> 4 slices of rye bread
> 4 big slices of ham
> 2 tsp Aleppo pepper

Remove any tough stems from the spinach. Rinse the spinach in plenty of cold water and drain. Heat 1 tbsp of the butter in a sauté pan, add the spinach and sauté for a few minutes, then drain again, to remove excess moisture.

Heat 2 tbsp more of the butter in a frying pan. Add the eggs and fry them over medium heat until the whites are firm and the yolks still soft. Remove from the heat.

Place the rye bread slices on a work top and spread some butter evenly on each slice. Divide the spinach between each bread slice, place a slice of ham on the spinach and a fried egg on top of that. Sprinkle with Aleppo pepper to serve.

# Waldorf salad

Some classic *smørrebrød* are borderline desserts. This recipe will often be served alongside other more savoury open sandwiches, but they are meant to be eaten last. *Serves 4*

100g (⅔ cup) green grapes
1 celery stick
1 head of chicory (endive)
30g (⅓ cup) walnuts
sea salt flakes and freshly ground black pepper
3–4 tbsp full-fat crème fraîche
1–2 tbsp lemon juice
4 slices of rye bread, plus 1 slice of toasted rye bread
salted butter

Halve the grapes and remove the seeds, if there are any. Cut the celery into thin slices on an angle. Cut the chicory into very thin slices. Chop the walnuts. Mix all together in a mixing bowl and season with salt and pepper. Gently fold in the crème fraîche and season with the lemon juice to taste.

Place the untoasted rye bread slices on a work top and spread the butter evenly on each slice. Divide the Waldorf salad between the slices. Crumble the toasted rye bread and place the rye crumbs on top.

**Variation:**
For a firmer texture, use Classic mayonnaise (see page 146) instead of crème fraîche.

# Frikadeller with sweet-and-sour pickles

*Frikadeller* (meatballs) is one of the most iconic Danish dishes. Meatballs are common to all cultures, but Danes think theirs are unique. Most families have their own recipe, so they will vary slightly. Often, I make them for dinner, then we have the leftovers the next day for lunch. For Christmas, we make them solely for the big lunch table prepared on Christmas Day.
*Serves 6*

> 9 Frikadeller (see page 168)
> 6 slices of rye bread
> salted butter
> 2 Pickled gherkins, sliced (see page 162)
> 2 dill sprigs
> 2 tsp Pesto (see page 156)
> parsley leaves
> 4 slices of Asier (see page 160)

**Variation:**
Instead of Pickled gherkins, use Sweet and sour cucumber (see page 163).

Cut the Frikadeller into halves. Place the rye bread slices on a work top and spread the butter evenly on each slice. Place 3 halves of Frikadeller on each slice of bread. Top 2 of the slices with Pickled gherkins and dill sprigs. Now divide the Pesto between 2 more open sandwiches and decorate with a couple of parsley leaves. Top the last 2 open sandwiches with Asier. Sprinkle with salt and pepper.

# Mackerel and tomato

This is a classic, but the mackerel almost always comes out of
a tin, which I intensely dislike for its taste, smell, and texture.
I have terrible memories of the smell in school classrooms, when
my fellow pupils would unwrap their lunch boxes with mackerel
in tomato sauce inside. So, whenever I eat mackerel with
tomato, it is always homemade. *Serves 4*

### for the tomato sauce
½ onion, finely chopped
1 garlic clove, finely chopped
1 tbsp olive oil
1 tbsp curry powder
1 tbsp caster (granulated) sugar
4 very ripe tomatoes, or 400g (14oz) can
    of chopped tomatoes
sea salt flakes and freshly ground
    black pepper
1 tbsp apple cider vinegar, or to taste

### for the smørrebrød
2 super fresh mackerel fillets
1 tbsp olive oil
6 slices of rye bread
salted butter
1 spring onion (scallion), cut into slices
    on an angle
2 tbsp roughly chopped parsley leaves

In a frying or sauté pan, sauté the onion and garlic in the olive
oil until softened. After a few minutes, add the curry powder
and sugar. Add the tomatoes, pour in 100ml (⅓ cup) water,
then season with salt and pepper. Let it simmer for 15 minutes,
then season to taste with vinegar, salt and pepper. Leave to cool
down a little.

Sprinkle the mackerel fillets with salt and pepper, then let
them rest for 30 minutes. Heat the oil in a frying pan and fry
the mackerel for 3–4 minutes on each side. Remove them from
the pan and remove the skin. Break the fish into large pieces.

Place the rye bread slices on a work top and spread the butter
evenly on each slice. Cut each bread slice into 2 triangles. Place
some mackerel on each triangle and top with 1 tbsp tomato
sauce. Decorate with the spring onion and parsley.

# Cottage cheese, peas, asparagus and chives

As a child, I never really cared for mayonnaise. Cottage cheese was my preferred topping, and when I started mixing my leftover vegetables with cottage cheese, it really was a revelation. Here is a tasty spring version. *Serves 4*

5 asparagus spears
200g (1½ cups) fresh peas, shelled
400g (1¾ cups) cottage cheese
8 tbsp finely chopped chives, plus 2 tbsp to serve
1–2 tbsp lemon juice
sea salt flakes and freshly ground black pepper
4 slices of rye bread
salted butter

Snap off the tough ends of the raw asparagus, then cut the spears into thin slices. Place them in a mixing bowl with the raw peas, cottage cheese and chives and mix well. Season to taste with lemon juice, salt and pepper.

   Place the rye bread slices on a work top and spread the butter evenly on each slice. Spread the cottage cheese mixture on each slice of bread. Sprinkle with chives and plenty of pepper.

**Variation:**
Cherry tomatoes and red onions could replace the green vegetables, and feel free to play around with the herbs you like.

# Chicken and pesto

Pesto is usually made with basil, but parsley is great as well (though I'm not sure if I should really be calling it pesto or salsa verde). I always have a lot of parsley because it is a big part of my everyday cooking, therefore I often use it for pesto, but you can easily mix in other herbs, such as dill, lovage or chervil. *Serves 4*

> 2–3 chicken breasts, or the equivalent in leftover chicken
> sea salt flakes and freshly ground black pepper
> salted butter or olive oil, for frying, plus salted butter
>     for the bread
> 4 slices of rye bread
> 4 lettuce leaves
> 4 tsp Pesto (see page 156)
> 1 red or green tomato, chopped

Sprinkle the chicken breast with salt and pepper. Heat the butter or oil in a frying pan and fry the chicken for 3–4 minutes on each side, or until cooked all the way through (cut one of the breasts open to test; it should have no trace of pink). Leave to cool down a little.

Place the rye bread slices on a work top and spread the butter evenly on each slice. Cut the chicken into pieces. Lay a lettuce leaf on top of each slice of rye bread, then the chicken. Add 1 tsp Pesto to each, then divide the tomato between the slices. Sprinkle with pepper to serve.

**Variation:**
Instead of the Pesto, you can use any mayonnaise you might have left over, mango chutney, or even cottage cheese.

# Æggekage baked eggs with tarragon and potatoes

*Æggekage* is an old Danish dish made from eggs with fried slices of salted pork belly. You can find recipes for this in cookbooks dating back to 1864, when it is said to have been served to soldiers fighting in the Danish-German war. I make my *æggekage* with leftover potatoes instead of pork belly and serve it with tomatoes and chives. *Serves 4*

20 cherry tomatoes on the vine
1 tbsp extra virgin olive oil
200g (7oz) cold, boiled potatoes, finely chopped
4 slices of rye bread
2 tbsp chives, chopped

**for the baked eggs**
8 large eggs
100ml (⅓ cup) single (light) cream
sea salt flakes and freshly ground black pepper
1 tsp salted butter
1 spring onion (scallion), finely sliced
2 tbsp finely chopped tarragon leaves

Preheat the oven to fan 180°C/400°F/gas 6.

Brush the tomatoes with olive oil, and bake in the oven for 10 minutes.

Meanwhile, beat the eggs well in a jug, then beat in the cream and add salt and pepper.

Melt the butter in a medium-sized frying pan that has a lid and sauté the spring onion, tarragon and potatoes for 3–4 minutes. Pour the egg mixture into the pan, reduce the heat and cover with the lid. Let it bake on the stove for 15 minutes. Or, if you use an ovenproof frying pan, the eggs can be finished in the oven alongside the tomatoes for about 10 minutes.

While they are still warm, cut the baked eggs into pieces and place them on the slices of rye bread. Sprinkle with the chives and serve right away with the baked tomatoes.

**Variation:**
This can also be served with crispy bacon crumbled on top.

# Chicken and minted pea purée

Often, I have a bit of chicken left over from dinner that I use up the next day for lunch. Here is a really delicious summer version, using fresh-cooked chicken breasts; obviously, you can swap in leftover roast chicken. *Serves 4*

### for the smørrebrød
2–3 chicken breasts, or the equivalent in leftover chicken
sea salt flakes and freshly ground black pepper
salted butter or olive oil, for frying, plus salted butter
    for the bread
4 slices of rye bread
4 small sprigs of coriander (cilantro)

### for the minted pea purée
200g (1½ cups) frozen peas
1–2 tbsp chopped mint leaves
3 tbsp olive oil
2 tbsp lemon juice

Sprinkle the chicken breast with salt and pepper. Heat the butter or oil in a frying pan and fry the chicken for 3–4 minutes on each side, or until cooked all the way through. Leave to cool down a little.

Defrost the peas, then blend to a purée in a food processor with the mint and olive oil; don't take it too far, though, as you want to keep some texture. Season to taste with lemon juice, salt and pepper.

Place the rye bread slices on a work top and spread butter evenly on each slice. Cut the chicken into slices. Place on the rye bread, then place about 2 tbsp of pea purée on each. Sprinkle with pepper and decorate each with a sprig of coriander.

# Peaches, blue cheese and balsamic syrup

These pieces of *smørrebrød* can be served on sourdough toast. Try the Sourdough loaf with spices (see page 143), baked with coriander and caraway seeds, which adds wonderfully to the sweet flavour of the peach. Or you can just buy a tasty regular sourdough loaf. *Serves 4*

1 tbsp honey
4 tbsp balsamic vinegar
4 peaches
2 tsp salted butter
4 slices of sourdough bread
50g (1¾oz) blue cheese
thyme or marjoram flowers (optional)

In a small saucepan, melt the honey, add the balsamic vinegar and let it simmer for 2–3 minutes.

Halve the peaches, remove the stones and cut them into wedges. In a frying pan, fry the wedges in the butter on both sides over a medium heat, until lightly brown.

Toast the bread, and place the peaches on the bread slices directly from the pan. Crumble the blue cheese and place it on top. Lightly sprinkle with the balsamic syrup and decorate with herb flowers (if using).

**Variation:**
Both Parmigiano Reggiano and cheddar can be used instead of blue cheese, if you prefer.

# Ham and scrambled egg in the Danish fashion

Pork has always been popular in Denmark, and the curing of ham has been going on for centuries. Traditional Danish ham is salted, then cooked. Here, the salty flavour from the ham is balanced by the eggs. *Serves 4*

### for the scrambled eggs

2 eggs
4 tbsp whole milk
sea salt flakes and freshly ground black pepper
1 tbsp salted butter

### for the smørrebrød

4 slices of sourdough or white bread
salted butter (optional)
4 big slices of cooked ham
4 tbsp watercress

Beat the eggs for 1 minute, then beat in the milk. Season with a little salt and some pepper. Melt the butter in a small heavy-based saucepan over a low heat. Pour the egg mixture into the pan and stir gently with a fork until the eggs are just set. Immediately place the scrambled eggs on a dish. Toast the slices of bread and place them on 4 plates, buttering them if you like.

Arrange the ham on the toasted bread, not flat, but so you get a bit of height. Divide the scrambled eggs on top and decorate with watercress.

# Mackerel rillettes

In August, the mackerel are big and fat, and that's when they are best to smoke. They can be eaten on rye bread with egg yolk and raw onions. When I visit my mother in the country in summertime, we always sit outside and eat this *smørrebrød*. I have merely added fresh coriander; I hope she doesn't mind... *Serves 4*

> 170g smoked mackerel
> 2 hard-boiled eggs, chopped (see page 145)
> 2 tbsp finely chopped chives
> 5 radishes, finely chopped
> 1 tbsp lemon juice
> 2 tbsp lime juice
> 1½ tsp finely grated unwaxed lime zest
> 2 tbsp chopped coriander (cilantro), plus leaves
>     to decorate
> 1½ tsp chilli flakes
> freshly ground black pepper
> 4 slices of rye bread
> salted butter

Carefully remove and discard the skin and bones from the mackerel. Break up the fish into pieces.

Mix the mackerel, eggs, chives, radishes, lemon juice, lime juice, lime zest, coriander and chilli flakes. Season to taste with pepper.

Place the rye bread slices on a work top and spread the butter evenly on each slice. Divide the Mackerel rillettes between each bread slice and top with the coriander leaves.

# Split pea cakes

These are my favourite veggie *frikadeller* – the Danish word for
meatballs which can be made from meat, fish or vegetables.
I often make these when I have people over for lunch. *Serves 4*

### for the split pea cakes
200g (1 generous cup) yellow
 split peas
1 carrot, coarsely grated
1 medium onion, chopped
2 tbsp chopped lovage, parsley
 or thyme
1 tsp coriander seeds, crushed
4 tbsp plain (all-purpose) flour
1 tbsp breadcrumbs
3 eggs, lightly beaten
sea salt flakes and freshly ground
 black pepper

2–3 tbsp olive oil
2 tbsp salted butter

### for the smørrebrød
4 slices of rye bread
salted butter
4 tbsp Rémoulade (see page 164)
4 tbsp Sweet and sour cucumber
 (see page 163)
1 sprig of chervil, or parsley, dill
 or chives

Soak the split peas in cold water overnight.

The next day, drain the peas. Place them in a saucepan and
cover with plenty of fresh water. Bring to the boil, then reduce
the heat, cover and let them simmer for about 30 minutes, until
tender. Drain them and let them cool a little.

Place the split peas, carrot and onion in a food processor and
blend to a coarse purée. Scrape the purée into a mixing bowl,
add the remaining ingredients, seasoning quite generously, and
stir until evenly mixed.

Heat the oil and butter in a frying pan. Take 1 tsp of the
mixture and fry it in a little oil to check if the mixture needs
more salt and pepper. Form little oval balls, each containing
about 1 tbsp of mixture. Fry on all sides over a medium heat for
about 15 minutes, until golden outside and cooked within.

Place the rye bread slices on a work top and spread the butter
evenly on each slice. Add 1½ still-warm frikadeller to each, then
add 1 tbsp of Rémoulade and Sweet and sour cucumber to each
slice. Sprinkle with chervil and serve straight away.

# Cod and potatoes

After cooking dinner, I often have a few leftovers; not enough for dinner the next day, but just enough for my lunch. This is not a classic, but one of my own ways of using fish and potatoes, inspired by *brandade. Serves 4*

300g (10½oz) cod fillet
sea salt flakes and freshly ground black pepper
3 medium-sized cold, boiled potatoes
2 tbsp olive oil
½ tsp freshly grated nutmeg
4 slices of rye bread
4 tbsp finely chopped radishes
4 tbsp finely chopped chives

Preheat the oven to 180°C/350°F/gas 4.

Place the cod in an ovenproof dish, sprinkle with salt and pepper and bake for 10 minutes. Cool down and carefully remove any bones you find.

Place the cod, potatoes, olive oil and nutmeg in a mixing bowl. Mash the cod mixture with a fork and mix it well together. Season to taste with salt and pepper.

Place the rye bread slices on a work top. Divide the cod and potato mix on each slice of bread, and place radishes and chives on top. Sprinkle with pepper.

# Fried fish with rémoulade and lemon

We have a lot of flatfish in Denmark – plaice is very popular – and we also have a lot of recipes for fried fish on rye bread. Here is one version with rémoulade and lemon. *Serves 4*

4 plaice fillets
100g (1 cup) breadcrumbs
sea salt flakes and freshly ground black pepper
50g (6 tbsp) plain (all-purpose) flour
2 eggs, lightly beaten
salted butter
4 slices of rye bread
4 tbsp Rémoulade (see page 164)
4 slices of lemon
4 small sprigs of dill

Cut each plaice fillet in half.

Mix the breadcrumbs with salt and pepper and spread them on a big plate. Place the flour on a second plate, then pour the eggs into a shallow dish.

Dredge each piece of plaice fillet through the flour and knock off the excess, then dip it in the beaten egg. Hold it up to drain off any excess egg, then place it in the breadcrumbs. Turn the fish over until the fillet is evenly coated with a good laycr of crumbs. Repeat with the other fillets. You can now put the breaded fillets into the fridge for at least 30 minutes to firm up the breadcrumbs, if you want.

Melt some butter in a frying pan. Fry the fish in the butter on both sides for 2–3 minutes.

Place the rye bread slices on a big platter and, when the fish is done, place 2 pieces of fillet on each piece. Add 1 tbsp Rémoulade on top and a lemon slice, sprinkle with pepper, decorate with a dill sprig and serve right away.

**Variation:**
Try this with Lemon mayonnaise (see page 149) and cooked prawns on top, too.

# Ham and Italian salad

It is hard to know why this topping is called Italian salad. Most food historians believe it is a reference to a European tradition of mixing mayonnaise with vegetables. A chef colleague and great friend of mine will always mention this piece of *smørrebrød* as her favourite, so if I omitted the recipe, I would disappoint her. Anyway, the Italian salad has to be home-made. *Serves 4*

### for the Italian salad

1 carrot, peeled
sea salt flakes
100g (⅔ cup) peas, fresh and shelled, or frozen
2 tbsp full-fat crème fraîche
1 tbsp Classic mayonnaise (see page 146)
1 tbsp Dijon mustard
freshly ground black pepper

### for the smørrebrød

4 slices of rye bread
salted butter
4 big slices of ham
8 tbsp Italian salad
3 tbsp chopped chervil leaves or flat-leaf parsley

Cut the carrot into small cubes, 1 x 1cm (⅜ x ⅜in). Boil them in lightly salted water for 5 minutes, then drain. Blanch the peas for 1 minute, then drain them, too.

Mix the crème fraîche, mayonnaise and Dijon mustard, add the drained carrots and peas and season with salt and pepper.

Place the rye bread slices on a work top and spread the butter evenly on each slice. Arrange a slice of ham over each, not flat, but so you get a bit of height. Place 2 tbsp Italian salad on each slice of ham, decorate with chervil and sprinkle with pepper.

# Roast beef – 2 ways

You can go to any butcher in Denmark and buy slices of roast beef; it makes a very popular *smørrebrød*. This recipe has many flavours going on: umami, sweet and spicy. If you go to any *smørrebrød* restaurant, you will get roast beef *smørrebrød* in a very elaborate style, with a lot of toppings. *Serves 4*

## Horseradish and Sweet and sour cucumber

4 slices of rye bread
salted butter
12 slices of roast beef
4 tbsp Horseradish cream
   (see page 163)
4 tbsp Sweet and sour cucumber
   (see page 163)
4 tbsp freshly grated horseradish
sea salt flakes and freshly ground
   black pepper

Place the rye bread slices on a work top and spread the butter evenly on each slice.

Arrange 3 slices of roast beef on each slice of bread, not flat, but so you get a bit of height. On each slice, place 1 tbsp Horseradish cream on one side of the meat, and on the other side place 1 tbsp Sweet and sour cucumber. Top with the grated horseradish and sprinkle with salt and pepper.

## Rémoulade and double onion

4 slices of rye bread
salted butter
12 slices of roast beef
4 tbsp Rémoulade (see page 164)
4 tbsp Sweet and sour cucumber
   (see page 163)
4 tbsp Crispy onions (see page 156)
sea salt flakes and freshly ground
   black pepper

Place the rye bread slices on a work top and spread the butter evenly on each slice.

Arrange 3 slices of roast beef on each slice of bread, not flat, but so you get a bit of height. On each slice, place 1 tbsp Rémoulade on one side of the meat, and on the other side place 1 tbsp Sweet and sour cucumber. Place 1 tbsp Crispy onions on top. Sprinkle with salt and pepper.

# Pickled herring – 3 ways

Herring for lunch is amazing and, in the dark Scandinavian winter, has the added benefit of being an important source of vitamin D. It's a very tedious process to make pickled herring, as they have to be salted for months, so I buy mine. *Serves 4*

12 slices of rye bread
salted butter

### Spiced

4 sweet and spicy red pickled
   herring fillets
2 hard-boiled eggs, sliced (see page 145)
2 tbsp cress

### Plain

4 plain pickled herring fillets
1 shallot, finely sliced
2 tbsp finely chopped chives

### Curried

4 plain pickled herring fillets
4 tbsp crème fraîche
1 tsp curry powder
1 apple, cut into cubes
1 tbsp capers, rinsed and drained
½ small red onion, finely sliced
1–2 tbsp lemon juice
sea salt flakes and freshly ground
   black pepper
2 tbsp finely chopped dill

First prepare the curried herrings. Cut the fillets into smaller pieces. Put the crème fraîche in a bowl and mix in the curry powder. Core the apple and cut it into small cubes, then mix it with the capers, onion and lemon juice. Season to taste. Add the herrings to the dressing and leave them in the fridge for at least 1 hour.

Place the rye bread slices on a cutting board and spread the butter evenly on each slice.

First divide the curried herring pieces over 4 slices of the bread. Decorate with dill.

For the spiced herrings, cut the red herrings into smaller pieces. Place the slices on 4 pieces of the bread, alternating with slices of egg, and top with cress.

Finally, for the plain herrings, cut the herrings into smaller pieces. Place the pieces on the remaining 4 slices of bread. Top each with 2–3 slices of shallot and sprinkle with the chives.

# Hummus, carrot, parsley and Parma ham

When I grew up in Copenhagen in the early 1970s, I was the only child to have hummus in my lunch box. I loved it, though my fellow pupils complained that I smelled of garlic! At that time, garlic was not common in Danish cuisine. *Serves 4*

### for the hummus
200g (1¼ cups) dried chickpeas
  (garbanzo beans)
4 tbsp tahini
juice of 1 lemon, or to taste
1–2 garlic cloves, crushed
sea salt flakes and freshly ground
  black pepper
pinch of ground cumin

### for the smørrebrød
4 slices of Parma ham
4 slices of rye bread
1 carrot, finely chopped
4 tbsp chopped parsley leaves

Put the chickpeas in a bowl and cover with twice their volume of cold water, then leave to soak overnight. The next day, drain the chickpeas, rinse well and put in a large saucepan with fresh water. Bring to the boil, then reduce the heat and simmer gently until they're tender; it will take 45 minutes to 1 hour. Leave them to cool in the water, then drain well, reserving the cooking liquid.

Mix the tahini with half the lemon juice and half the garlic, then put this in a food processor with the chickpeas. Whizz to make a purée. Now gradually pour in enough of the chickpea cooking water to give a soft paste that will hold its shape. Season to taste with salt and pepper, cumin and more garlic or lemon juice. Cover, and keep in the refrigerator for up to a week.

For the *smørrebrød*, in a dry pan, fry the Parma ham on each side until crisp. Leave to cool, then crumble it. Place the rye bread slices on a work top and cut each into 2 triangles, then spread hummus evenly on each slice. Divide the carrot between the triangles, then sprinkle with the Parma ham. Decorate each slice with parsley and sprinkle with pepper.

**Variation:**
This can also be served with slices of tomato, cucumber and red (bell) pepper on top of the hummus.

# Salmon, egg and basil

I often serve open sandwiches as a starter or snack with white wine before dinner. They are also great at teatime instead of finger sandwiches. Easy-to-do and tasty, salmon is always a winner. If you do not want to cure your own salmon, use high-quality smoked salmon instead. *Serves 4*

> 4 big slices of sourdough bread
> salted butter
> 8 lettuce leaves, or mustard greens
> 8–16 slices of Quick-cured salmon (see page 150)
> 2 hard-boiled eggs (see page 145)
> 1 tbsp chopped dill
> sea salt flakes and freshly ground black pepper
> 4 cherry tomatoes
> 4 basil leaves

Toast the sourdough slices, then spread each slice with a thin layer of butter, cut in half and place on a work top.

Lay a lettuce leaf on each slice of bread, followed by 1 or 2 slices of salmon, depending on their size, but erring on the side of generosity.

Chop the eggs in a small mixing bowl and mix them with the dill, salt and pepper, then place on top of the salmon. Quarter the tomatoes and place on top of the eggs, then decorate each with a basil leaf.

# Rullepølse and beer jelly

*Rullepølse* can be served in many ways and a traditional favourite is with beef jelly on top, which you can buy from all Danish butchers. I like to tweak this classic, making a jelly out of beer with a more bitter-sweet flavour, perfect with *Rullepølse*. Make the jelly the day before, as it takes some time to set. *Serves 4*

### for the beer jelly
2 gelatine leaves (about 4g)
200ml (7fl oz) IPA
1 tsp finely grated unwaxed lemon zest

### for the smørrebrød
4 slices of rye bread
salted butter
8 slices of Rullepølse (see page 171)
1 small onion, finely sliced into rings
handful of cress

Soften the gelatine leaves in cold water for 5–10 minutes. Take the leaves out of the water and squeeze them hard with your hands, then melt in a small saucepan over a low heat (be careful not to get the gelatine too hot, or it won't set properly).

When melted, mix with the beer and lemon zest, then pour into a small container or bowl. Place in the refrigerator until it has set; this will take 6–8 hours, or overnight.

Place the rye bread slices on a work top and spread the butter evenly on each slice. Place 2 slices of *Rullepølse* on each slice of bread. Chop the beer jelly into small cubes and place on the *Rullepølse*, add onion rings, then decorate with cress.

# Amagermad – cheese
# and 2 kinds of bread

A standard for sandwiches to go – easy to carry with you when you are too busy for breakfast or lunch. The two different kinds of breads work perfectly together, and are also great for a lunch box. *Serves 4*

4 slices of rye bread
4 slices of white bread
salted butter
8 slices of cheese

Place all the bread slices on a work top and spread the butter evenly on each slice. Place 2 slices of cheese on the white bread and place the rye bread on top. Serve with tea or coffee.

# Special

*Smørrebrød* is a very specific Danish food culture. It's our contribution to the world of food, something we can be proud of.

And, though it looks simple, *smørrebrød* has to be made with the best ingredients and a great deal of care and thought. The toppings must have different textures and combinations of flavours. If you get it right, nothing beats it.

While *smørrebrød* is most often an everyday lunch on the go, it can also be a more elaborate affair, eaten for lunch at a restaurant, or made from scratch in a home kitchen. Being invited for a weekend lunch of *smørrebrød* is a real treat.

I love inviting people over for *smørrebrød*. Since I was a tiny child – and still today – we have had people over for what is called 'the big cold table', a large buffet of toppings to put on rye bread. You choose your toppings, then sit down, make your *smørrebrød* and eat for hours. If you're ever invited to one of these, there is a rule to observe: you start with fish – usually herring – then move on to vegetables and meat, and finish with cheese. If you want to hold one of these lunches, aim for two or three pieces of *smørrebrød* per person. Place the toppings on a big serving tray and let your guests dig in. It is great fun. But you can also make the *smørrebrød* for your guests if you prefer: an amazing treat, probably pure love!

There are different *smørrebrød* for every season and each mood. In winter you can enjoy herring, then duck with chicory and apple (see page 120), then salted beef with horseradish (see page 134). For summer, you might opt for prawns, then soft leeks with eggs and vinaigrette. Just one or two make a loving Sunday supper – I often eat this with my husband – served with a glass of wine.

# Heirloom tomatoes with tarragon mayo

This is a classic summer *smørrebrød*. During the summer, when the tomatoes are ripe, this is an absolute favourite among Danes. It's important to sprinkle a little salt on top, to enhance the juicy flavour of the tomato. I always eat this one at my mother's house, with the tomatoes fresh out of her greenhouse. *Serves 4*

> 4 slices of rye bread
> salted butter
> 10–12 tomatoes – green, red and orange
> sea salt flakes and freshly ground black pepper
> 4 tbsp Tarragon mayonnaise (see page 148)
> 1 spring onion (scallion), finely sliced
> small handful of finely chopped tarragon leaves

Place the rye bread slices on a work top and spread the butter evenly on each slice. Cut the tomatoes into slices and place 8–9 slices, overlapping, on each slice of rye bread. Sprinkle with salt and pepper.

Place 1 tbsp Tarragon mayonnaise on top of each, then decorate with spring onion and tarragon.

**Variation:**
Serve with bacon on top, use cottage cheese instead of mayonnaise, or even Horseradish cream or Pesto (see pages 163 and 156).

# Leek and egg

A summer classic. Nothing is better than cooking with the ingredients the season offers you. The best leeks I've ever had were from my mother's garden, freshly pulled up from the ground, cleaned, and cooked. This is great for lunch, or as a starter. *Serves 4*

## for the vinaigrette

2 tsp Dijon mustard
2 tbsp white wine vinegar
½ tsp honey
sea salt flakes and freshly ground
    black pepper
5 tbsp extra virgin olive oil

## for the smørrebrød

3 thin leeks
5 slices of rye bread
2 tbsp capers, drained and rinsed
1–2 tsp salted butter
2 hard-boiled eggs (see page 145)
1 tbsp finely chopped chives
leaves from 4 sprigs of chervil or
    flat-leaf parsley

Start with the vinaigrette. Whisk together the mustard, vinegar, honey, salt and pepper in a small bowl, then whisk constantly while drizzling in the oil. Taste and adjust the seasoning, if necessary.

Cut each leek into 3–4 pieces, each about 5cm (2in) long. Rinse them well in cold water, then steam them over salted boiling water for 2–3 minutes. Drain and dry them, then halve the pieces lengthways.

Take 1 slice of rye bread and crumble it into small crumbs. Place in a dry frying pan over a medium-high heat and toast the crumbs, stirring, until crisp. Fry the capers in the butter until they open up like little flowers, then leave them in the pan.

Place the 4 rye bread slices on plates and divide the steamed leeks between them. Chop the eggs and spread them over the leeks. Add the fried capers and toasted rye crumbs, then sprinkle with chives and black pepper. Drizzle the dressing over the whole dish, then decorate with chervil.

# Avocado, asparagus and poached egg

Avocado on rye – instead of on the ubiquitous Instagram toast – is a Scandi touch. The love of avocado seems to have exploded. Here is a slightly upscaled version that I love to make on late weekend mornings. *Serves 4*

6 asparagus spears
sea salt flakes
2 avocados
4 slices of rye bread
salted butter
4 eggs
1 tbsp Aleppo pepper
4 tbsp cress, or chervil leaves

Snap off the tough ends of the asparagus, then cut the spears into 3 pieces. Blanch them in salted boiling for 1 minute, then drain them, slice each piece lengthways and leave to cool down.

Cut each avocado in half, remove the stones, then peel and slice them.

Place the rye bread slices on a work top and spread the butter evenly on each slice. Place the asparagus on the bread, then the avocado slices.

Poach the eggs, according to your preferred method (see page 145). Place an egg on top of each sandwich. Sprinkle with Aleppo pepper and decorate with cress or chervil.

# Salmon on sourdough

Although it's quintessentially Scandinavian, we only had salmon as a starter for special occasions when I was growing up, or at Christmas lunch. You can do a quick-cured salmon instead of the three-day process needed for gravadlax – so easy for *smørrebrød* toppings. This will make me happy any day. *Serves 4*

> 4 slices of Sourdough loaf with spices (see page 143)
> 8 slices of Quick-cured salmon (see page 150)
> ⅓ cucumber, finely chopped
> 4 tbsp Horseradish cream (see page 163)
> 4 tbsp freshly grated horseradish
> freshly ground black pepper
> 4 sprigs of dill

Toast the bread slices and place on 4 plates, then place 2 salmon slices on each piece. Divide the cucumber between the pieces, then add 1 tbsp Horseradish cream to each. Decorate with grated horseradish, sprinkle with pepper and add a sprig of dill.

**Variation:**
If you're not feeling as though the task of baking bread is possible, buy a good-quality sourdough bread instead. Good-quality smoked salmon can be used instead of home-cured.

# Fried herrings in brine

It can be difficult to get good-quality pickled herring. This recipe is the perfect alternative, and it's not hard to make. Your fishmonger will be able to get you ultra-fresh herrings. *Serves 4*

### for the brine
300ml (1¼ cups) distilled (clear) vinegar
150g (¾ cup) caster (granulated) sugar
1 tbsp peppercorns
1 tbsp yellow mustard seeds
1 bay leaf

sea salt flakes and freshly ground
   black pepper
4 tsp Dijon mustard
4 tsp finely chopped dill
30g (3½ tbsp) salted butter
1 red onion, sliced

### for the herring
8 fresh herring fillets
150g (1 cup) rye flour

### for the smørrebrød
4 slices of rye bread
salted butter
4 sprigs of dill

Combine all the ingredients for the brine in a saucepan and bring to the boil, then reduce the heat and leave to simmer for 30 minutes. Remove from the heat and set aside to cool.

To prepare the herring, cut off the fins and rinse. Mix the rye flour with salt and pepper. Press the herring fillets skin-side down in the flour, to coat. In a small bowl, mix the mustard and dill. Spread 1 tsp of the mustard mixture over the flesh side of each herring and fold it over to cover; each fillet will form a square sandwich, with the mustard in the centre. Once more, make sure the skin is covered with rye flour.

Heat the butter in a frying pan and cook the herrings for 3–5 minutes on each side, depending on their size. Place the cooked herrings in a large plastic box, laying them side by side. Scatter the sliced onion over the herrings and cover with the brine. Leave to marinate for 2 hours. (These will keep, in the brine, for up to 1 week.)

Take out the fish and let each fillet dry a little. For the *smørrebrød*, place the rye bread slices on a work top and spread the butter evenly on each slice. Place a marinated herring on each slice and decorate with marinated onion and the dill.

# Cod and fennel

In Denmark, we have a traditional dish with fried plaice and prawns that we call 'shooting star'. Sometimes you have to stir up the classics a little bit, so I came up with this; I hope I've created a new classic! *Serves 4*

> 1 fennel bulb
> 500g (1lb 2oz) cod fillet
> 1 egg
> 100g (1¼ cups) breadcrumbs
> sea salt flakes and freshly ground black pepper
> 5 slices of rye bread
> 2 tbsp capers, drained and rinsed
> 1 tsp salted butter, plus more for the capers
> 4 tbsp Lemon mayonnaise (see page 149)
> 1 tbsp finely grated unwaxed lemon zest
> 1 bunch of watercress

Cut the fennel in very thin slices, using a mandolin if you have one, and place in a bowl with ice-cold water.

Cut the cod into 8 pieces, as even as possible. Lightly beat the egg and place in a shallow dish. Mix the breadcrumbs with salt and pepper and place in a second dish. Dip each piece of cod in the egg, then hold it up to drain off any excess. Now turn the fish over in the breadcrumbs until well coated, then place on a sheet of baking parchment. Repeat with the remaining pieces.

Take 1 slice of rye bread and crumble it into small crumbs. Place in a dry frying pan over a medium-high heat and toast the crumbs, stirring, until crisp. Fry the capers in a little butter until they open up like little flowers, then leave them in the pan.

Now fry the breaded cod fillets in the remaining butter, in batches if necessary, for 2–3 minutes on each side until really crisp, making sure the pan is never dry. Place 2 cod pieces on each slice of rye bread, add the Lemon mayonnaise, then drain the fennel well and place on top of the cod with the lemon zest. Sprinkle with the toasted crumbs and capers and serve warm, topped with the watercress.

**Variation:**
Serve with Tarragon mayonnaise (see page 148), capers and sliced tomatoes.

# Freshwater prawns on sourdough caraway bread

Most *smørrebrød* is served with rye bread, but there are exceptions and one of them is for these prawns from fjords: they always come on sourdough. Their season is short, and different from year to year. They are very expensive, but less so if you peel them yourself. So, once or twice every summer, I treat myself to them for lunch. I bake the sourdough with caraway seeds, then relax and enjoy my special meal. *Serves 4*

2 lemons
400g (14oz) freshwater prawns (shrimp)
1 tbsp lemon juice
sea salt flakes and freshly ground black pepper
4 slices of Sourdough loaf with spices (see page 143)
salted butter
4 tbsp Classic mayonnaise (see page 146)
2 tbsp grated unwaxed lemon zest
4 sprigs of dill

Cut the lemons in half and wrap each piece in muslin.

Place the prawns in a bowl, then season to taste with lemon juice, salt and pepper.

Place the bread slices on a work top and spread the butter evenly on each slice, then divide the prawns between the slices. Place 1 tbsp Classic mayonnaise on top of each, then sprinkle with pepper. Decorate with lemon zest and dill and serve with the halved lemons.

# Smoked herring and egg yolk

Imagine a warm summer's day. You are sitting on a pier in a harbour, there's a light breeze and the sound of the water slowly swashing against the pier's pillars, and birdsong twitters in the background. That's a Danish summer. And so is this freshly smoked herring with rye bread, egg yolk and ice-cold beer. It's a famous dish on Bornholm, the Danish island in the Baltic Sea, which has renowned smokehouses. *Serves 4*

> 4 smoked herrings
> salted butter
> 4 slices of rye bread
> 8 cherry tomatoes
> 4 egg yolks
> 8 radishes, chopped
> 2 tbsp finely chopped chives
> 2 tbsp finely chopped parsley leaves
> freshly ground black pepper

Carefully remove the skin and bones from the herrings and break up the meat into smaller pieces.

Spread the butter on the rye bread slices and place them on plates. Place the pieces of herring on each slice of bread.

Cut the tomatoes into small wedges and place them on top of the herring and around the bread. Place a raw egg yolk in the middle of each piece, then sprinkle with radishes, chives and parsley. Lastly, scatter with plenty of pepper.

**Variation:**
Instead of smoked herring you can use smoked mackerel.

**115**

# Chicken salad

Another perfect leftover recipe which gives you an excellent new meal to enjoy. If you do not have white asparagus, then use leftover vegetables, such as mushrooms or cucumber, instead.
*Serves 4*

350g (12oz) cooked chicken, or fresh chicken breasts
a little flavourless oil (optional)
sea salt flakes and freshly ground black pepper
200g (7oz) white asparagus spears
1 small celery stick, finely chopped
1 tbsp finely chopped tarragon leaves
2 tbsp capers, drained and rinsed
4 tbsp Classic mayonnaise (see page 146)
2 tbsp crème fraîche or natural yogurt
2 tsp lemon juice, or to taste
4 slices of rye bread, toasted
watercress, to serve

If you are using fresh chicken breasts, fry them in a little oil for 4–5 minutes on each side, or until cooked through, then sprinkle with salt and pepper and leave to cool. Pull the cooked chicken off the bone and then into smaller pieces.

Break off the lower third of the asparagus; keep this for making soup, as it's tough. Peel the raw stalks below the tips, then thinly slice.

Mix the chicken, asparagus, celery, tarragon and capers in a bowl. Add the Classic mayonnaise, crème fraîche and lemon juice, then season with salt and pepper and fold everything together gently. Taste and adjust the levels of lemon juice, salt and pepper, if you like.

Serve the chicken salad with toasted rye bread and watercress.

# Beef tartare

Once in a while, I get a real craving for tartare on rye bread.
When it happens, I visit my local organic butcher and have
him carve out some really nice beef for me. I bicycle home
and make *smørrebrød* in my kitchen, and serve it with ice-cold
pilsner. Taking time on Saturday to have a lunch like this is real
downtime for me. *Serves 4*

> 8 medium-sized potatoes
> about 500ml (2 cups) flavourless oil
> sea salt flakes
> 4 slices of rye bread
> salted butter
> 400g (14oz) very good-quality steak tartare,
>     from your butcher
> 4 tsp finely chopped shallots
> 2 tbsp capers, drained and rinsed
> 4 tsp cress
> freshly ground black pepper
> 4 egg yolks

Slice the potatoes about 3mm (⅛in) thick and put in a large
bowl. Rinse in cold water until the water runs clear, then leave
to soak for 30 minutes.

Heat the oil in a deep pan. Drain the potatoes and dry really
well with kitchen paper. Fry them, in batches, until golden and
crisp, lifting them out with a slotted spoon or spider, so the oil
can run off quickly. Drain on kitchen paper and season lightly
with salt.

Place the rye bread slices on a work top and spread the butter
evenly on each slice. Slice 4 rectangles from the meat to fit the
bread as far as possible and place one on each slice, then sprinkle
with the shallots, capers, cress and pepper. Top with the potato
crisps. Serve with a raw egg yolk.

# Duck, chicory and apple

This one is a real winter *smørrebrød*. Chicory is called 'Christmas salad' in Danish, so I only ever ate it at Christmastime as a child. Now I see it for sale all year round, but I only eat it in winter. Here it is packed with warm flavours for those dark winter days. *Serves 4*

### for the duck and cure
2 duck legs
1 tbsp sea salt flakes
1 tbsp caster (granulated) sugar
1 tsp coarsely ground black pepper
1 tbsp coriander seeds
½ tbsp chilli flakes

### for the smørrebrød
2 heads of chicory (endive)
2 apples
1 onion
sea salt flakes and freshly ground
   black pepper
4 slices of rye bread
salted butter

Slash the duck legs on both sides. Mix the salt, sugar and spices and rub them into the duck legs. Cover and leave in the fridge overnight.

The next day, preheat the oven to 180°C/350°F/gas 4.

Place the duck legs in an ovenproof dish and braise in the oven for 1½ hours. When cool enough to handle, pull the meat gently off the bone, reserving the fat.

Cut the chicory, apples and onion into wedges. Take some of the fat rendered by the duck legs from their dish, add it to a large frying pan, then use it to fry the apple and vegetables on all sides until golden brown. Turn off the heat under the pan and mix in the pieces of duck.

Place the rye bread slices on a work top and spread the butter evenly on each slice, then place all the warm vegetables and duck pieces on each slice. Serve right away.

# Christmas herring

Certain spices have a special connection with Christmas. Here is my spiced herring recipe that I serve on Christmas Day with rye bread. *Serves 4*

8 herring fillets
150g (1 cup) rye flour
sea salt flakes and freshly ground
 black pepper
salted butter

1½ tbsp coriander seeds, crushed
2 cloves
3 bay leaves
1 tsp mustard seeds
1 red onion, sliced

### for the brine
500ml (2 cups) distilled (clear) vinegar
300g (1½ cups) caster (granulated) sugar
1 tbsp allspice berries, crushed

### to serve
1 orange, segmented
4 slices of rye bread

Combine all the ingredients for the brine in a saucepan and bring to the boil, then reduce the heat and leave to simmer for 10 minutes. Remove from the heat and set aside to cool.

To prepare the herring, cut off the fins and rinse. Fold each fillet in half lengthways, skin side out. Mix the rye flour with salt and pepper. Press the herring fillets skin-side down in the flour, to coat.

Heat the butter in a frying pan and cook the herrings for 3–5 minutes on each side, depending on their size. Place the cooked herrings in a large plastic box, laying them side by side. Scatter the sliced onion over them and cover with the brine. Leave to marinate for 2 hours. (These will keep, in the brine, for up to 1 week.)

Take out the fish and let each fillet dry a little. Place on a serving dish with the marinated onion and orange segments and serve, with the rye bread on the side.

# Summer pork belly

Pork belly has got rather a lot of fat secreted between the layers of meat, but that makes it a perfect foil for redcurrant and vegetables in vinegar brine, both of which are good with sweet and fatty flavours. All in all, this recipe is a perfectly balanced combination of flavours. A glass of beer with it will not hurt.
*Serves 8*

> 800g (1lb 12oz) pork belly, skin-on (for crisp crackling)
> sea salt flakes and freshly ground black pepper
> 2 bay leaves
> 6 whole cloves
> 8 slices of rye bread
> 8 tbsp Shaken redcurrants (see page 159)
> 8 tbsp Sweet and sour cucumber (see page 163)

Preheat the oven to 200°C/400°F/gas 6.

Make sure the pork skin is scored well, cut through the skin down into the fat, and rub in salt and pepper. Place it in a roasting tray, then stick the bay leaves and cloves in the scored skin. Roast for 1 hour, then check its internal temperature: it should be 58°C (136°F); if not, roast a bit more.

Remove from the oven and leave to rest for 15 minutes, then carve the pork into slices. Place on the rye bread, then add 1 tbsp Shaken redcurrants to each, with 1 tbsp Sweet and sour cucumber. Sprinkle with pepper and serve right away.

**Variation:**
You could use redcurrant jelly instead of Shaken redcurrants, or even Sautéed red cabbage (see page 168).

**125**

# Creamy mushrooms on toast

This is a classic autumn treat. You can use any kind of mushroom all through the year, or dried mushrooms. However, in my opinion, nothing beats the autumn chanterelles or ceps... except mushrooms you forage for yourself! I serve this for lunch at weekends when the landscape is starting to change to brown, red and orange, the light is becoming ever so slightly warmer, and it is time to withdraw indoors. *Serves 4*

600g (1lb 5oz) mushrooms
300g (10½oz) chanterelles, or just regular mushrooms
1 tbsp salted butter
4 sprigs of thyme, plus thyme flowers, to serve (optional)
zest of ½ unwaxed lemon, grated
juice of ½–1 lemon
100ml (⅓ cup) single (light) cream
½ tsp freshly ground nutmeg
sea salt flakes and freshly ground black pepper
4 slices of Sourdough loaf with spices (see page 143)

Clean the mushrooms and cut them into quarters. Clean the chanterelles, but keep them dry.

Melt the butter in a large frying pan; there needs to be plenty of room for the mushrooms, otherwise they tend to boil instead of fry. Sauté both kinds of mushroom together with the sprigs of thyme until golden brown. Add the lemon zest and juice, cream and nutmeg and let it simmer for 2–3 minutes. Season to taste with salt and pepper.

While the mushrooms are cooking, toast the sourdough slices. Place them on plates and divide the creamy mushrooms between each slice. Decorate with thyme flowers, if you have them, and serve right away.

# Pariserbøf

Despite the name, this dish has nothing to do with Paris. It probably comes from an era when a lot of dishes were named after something French in order to be considered sophisticated! It's another Danish classic, usually served on white toast. I prefer it on rye bread, and so I never order it when I go out for lunch; I always make it at home. This piece of *smørrebrød* definitely deserves a cold beer. *Serves 4*

**for the pariserbøf**
500g (1lb 2oz) minced (ground) lean beef
150g (5½oz) beetroot, shredded
1 small red onion, about 25g (1oz)
4 tbsp capers, drained and rinsed
sea salt flakes and freshly ground black pepper
salted butter, for frying

**for the smørrebrød**
4 slices of rye bread
salted butter
4 tbsp Mustard pickles (see page 164)
4 tbsp Sweet and sour cucumber (see page 163)
freshly grated horseradish
4 egg yolks

Mix the beef with the beetroot, red onion and capers, then season with salt and pepper. Form it into 4 round patties. Melt the butter in a frying pan and fry the patties for 2–3 minutes on each side; the meat should still be rare to medium-rare inside.

Place the rye bread slices on a work top and spread the butter evenly on each slice. Place a beef patty on each piece, then 1 tbsp each of Mustard pickles, Sweet and sour cucumber and grated horseradish. Sprinkle with pepper and serve with a raw egg yolk on the side.

**Variation:**
Serve with a spicy chutney instead of the Mustard pickles.

# Christmas pork and red cabbage

It would not be Christmas without this. On the day after the Scandinavian Christmas Eve feast, I always have a lot of lovely leftovers, including roast pork on rye bread with red cabbage. Leftovers are often the best meals. *Serves 4*

> 4 slices of rye bread
> 8 slices of Roasted pork (see page 168), with crackling
> 200g (7oz) Sautéed red cabbage (see page 168)
> sea salt flakes and freshly ground black pepper

Place the rye bread slices on 4 plates, then add 2 slices of Roasted pork to each.

Warm up the Sautéed red cabbage and place 2–3 tbsp on each, then scatter the crisp crackling on top. Sprinkle with salt and pepper and serve.

**Variation:**
This also tastes amazing with a small spoonful of Horseradish cream (see page 163).

# Æbleflæsk Christmas pork belly with apple

*Æbleflæsk*, literally 'apple and pork belly', is another Christmas classic. There are a lot of regional recipes for this, and this version is not how my family would cook it; it's a more modern dish. *Serves 4*

8 slices of pork belly
1 tbsp sea salt flakes and freshly ground black pepper
3 Bramley apples (they must be tart)
2 red onions
2 celery sticks
1 tbsp mustard seeds
10 sprigs of thyme
4 slices of rye bread

Sprinkle the pork slices with the salt and pepper and leave to rest, covered, in the fridge, for 3–4 hours.

When you're ready to cook, preheat the oven to 180°C/350°F/gas 4.

Cut the apples and onions into wedges and place them on a baking sheet lined with baking parchment. Cut the celery into slices on an angle and mix them in, with the mustard seeds and thyme. Place the pork slices on top.

Cook in the oven for about 20 minutes, then turn each slice of pork, so it gets crisp on both sides, and return to the oven for another 20 minutes.

When done, take out of the oven, immediately place a bit of everything on the rye bread and serve right away.

# Salted beef with horseradish

Preparing the meat here is a lengthy process – I won't lie. Cooking, for me, is relaxing; I like to make things that take days and put lots of thought into the preparation. For me, it's about reclaiming time: who decided that everything must be so fast? You can also eat the beef for dinner with potatoes, Horseradish cream (see page 163) and steamed vegetables. *Serves 4*

### for the brine and beef
200g (7oz) salt
50g (¼ cup) caster (granulated) sugar
1 tbsp black peppercorns
3 bay leaves
1kg (2lb 4oz) beef brisket

### for the stock
1 onion
1 carrot
2 bay leaves
10 sprigs of thyme
10 peppercorns

### for the smørrebrød
4 slices of rye bread
salted butter
4 tbsp Horseradish cream
  (see page 163)
4 tbsp freshly grated horseradish
4 sprigs of chervil or flat-leaf parsley

Put all the brine ingredients (not the beef) into a large pan and pour in 1 litre (4¼ cups) water. Bring to the boil, then simmer until the salt and sugar have dissolved. Remove from the heat, leave to cool, then pour into a bowl. Add the beef to the cold brine, making sure it is completely covered (use a heavy object to keep it submerged) and refrigerate overnight.

The next day, drain the beef from the brine and place it in a stockpot with all the ingredients for the stock. Cover with 3 litres (3 quarts) water. Bring to the boil, skimming off any froth from the surface, then reduce to a simmer. Half-cover the pan and cook gently for 2 hours, then let the beef cool down in the stock. Take it out, cut the slices you need and keep the rest in the fridge for up to 7 days.

Place the rye bread slices on a work top and spread the butter evenly on each slice. Place the beef slices on the rye bread, then add 1 tbsp Horseradish cream to each piece. Top with the grated horseradish, pepper and chervil.

**Variation:**
Instead of horseradish, you can serve this with pickles and Sweet and sour cucumber (see page 163).

# Basics

To make *smørrebrød*, you need a few basic ingredients, all of which are a given in most Danish cupboards or refrigerators – some home-made, others shop-bought.

Most crucially, you need rye bread. Of course, it is possible to buy rye bread, but nothing beats the home-baked kind (see page 138). Rye bread in Denmark is a staple like milk, butter and cheese.

All the pickles and condiments, such as mayonnaise (see page 146), can be bought in shops, but they taste so much better when they are home-made; another bonus is that they will contain no preservatives.

Then there are the different meats, such as the *frikadeller* (see page 168), which are quite easy to make; liver pâté (see page 153), which always tastes very good and can easily be frozen; and the *rullepølse* (see page 171), which is a project in itself to make as it will stretch over a couple of days, but it is worth it because it tastes so good.

It is important to remember that you do not need to do all of this to make and eat *smørrebrød*; you can of course buy some of the things ready made, or use alternative ingredients. Think about it like LEGO: it is about using whichever pieces you already have to build your house.

So, essentially, bake good bread and then get started. Maybe make the mayonnaise and crispy onions (see page 156), too, and you will already have come a long way. There are, I believe, some great recipes in this chapter, so you should feel inspired to bring *smørrebrød* into your everyday life for health, taste and joy.

# Trine's rye bread

My classic rye bread. I always have it in my bread basket and I eat it every day. *Makes 1 large loaf*

### for the rye sourdough starter
300ml (1¼ cups) buttermilk
300g (2¼ cups) wholegrain
    stoneground rye flour

### for the rye bread:
### day 1
1 new rye sourdough starter,
    or 3 tbsp rye sourdough
    starter (see method below)
850ml (3½ cups) lukewarm water
15g (3 tbsp) sea salt flakes
750g (5⅔ cups) wholegrain
    stoneground rye flour
### day 2
500g (1lb 2oz) cracked rye
250ml (1 cup) cold water
a little flavourless oil, for the loaf tin

For the rye sourdough starter, mix the buttermilk and rye flour well in a bowl. Cover and leave at room temperature for 3 days. It's important that it doesn't turn mouldy, but starts bubbling; a temperature of 23–25°C (73–77°F) is ideal for this.

### day 1
If making your first loaf from the starter, dissolve all the starter in the lukewarm water in a large bowl (for the next loaf use just 3 tbsp of the starter that you will reserve on Day 2; the whole quantity of starter is just for the first attempt, and the loaf will be a little bigger). Stir in the salt and flour, cover the bowl with a towel and leave at room temperature for 12–24 hours.

### day 2
Add the cracked rye and cold water to the dough mixture and stir with a wooden spoon until smooth. It will be too runny to knead with your hands.

Remove 3 tbsp of the dough, place it in an airtight container and refrigerate; this will become your starter for the next loaf you make (it needs to rest for at least 3 days before using, and will last up to 8 weeks).

Lightly oil a large loaf tin, about 30 x 10cm (12 x 4in) and 10cm (4in) deep. Pour in the dough, cover with a damp towel and leave to rise for 3–6 hours until the dough has almost reached the top of the tin.

When ready to bake, preheat the oven to fan 180°C/400°F/gas 6. Bake the loaf for 1 hour 45 minutes, then immediately turn it out on to a wire rack to cool. This is great just out of the oven, but as it's difficult to cut, it's better the next day... if you can wait!

# Malted rye bread

Made with malt syrup, this is sweet and soft. *Makes 1 large loaf*

**day 1**
1 new rye sourdough starter, or 3 tbsp
    rye sourdough starter (see page 138)
600ml (2½ cups) lukewarm water
250g (2 cups) wholegrain stoneground
    rye flour
250g (1¾ cups) white strong
    (bread) flour

100g (¾ cup) linseeds (flaxseeds)
2 tbsp barley malt syrup
10g (2½ tsp) sea salt flakes
a little flavourless oil

**day 2**
350g (12oz) cracked rye
100ml (⅓ cup) water

**day 1**

If making your first loaf from the starter, dissolve all the starter in the lukewarm water in a large bowl (for the next loaf use just 3 tbsp of the starter that you will reserve on Day 2; the whole quantity of starter is just for the first attempt, and the loaf will be a little bigger). Stir in the rye flour, bread flour, linseeds, malt syrup and salt. Cover the bowl with a towel and leave at room temperature for 12–24 hours.

**day 2**

Add the cracked rye and water to the dough mixture and stir with a wooden spoon until smooth. It will be too runny to knead with your hands. Take out 3 tbsp of dough, place it in an airtight container and refrigerate; this will become your starter for the next loaf you make (it will need to rest for at least 3 days before you use it, and will last up to 8 weeks).

Lightly oil a large loaf tin, about 30 x 10cm (12 x 4in) and 10cm (4in) deep. Pour in the dough, cover with a damp towel and leave to rise for 3–6 hours, or until the dough has almost reached the top of the tin.

When ready to bake, preheat the oven to fan 180°C/400°F/ gas 6. Bake the loaf for 1 hour 15 minutes, then immediately turn it out on to a wire rack to cool. This is great just out of the oven, but as it's difficult to cut, it's better the next day.

# Biga

If you do not have a biga (a kind of pre-fermentation), you have to make it and it will take about 10 days. *Makes enough for 1 household biga*

>   150g (5½oz) white strong (bread)
>       flour, plus enough to feed the
>       biga for 7–10 days
>   100g (3½oz) wholemeal strong
>       (bread) flour
>   450ml (16fl oz) water

Measure the flours into a large mixing bowl. Gradually pour in the water, mixing with your hand or a whisk, until it is the consistency of pancake batter.

Every day, discard 80 per cent of the biga, add about as much water and both of the flours to make up the difference (it's impossible to be exact about quantities, you'll have to use your judgement) and mix well. Do this every day for 7–10 days until the biga comes to life: you will notice small bubbles or a sour smell. Now it's ready.

You have to keep 'feeding' the biga like this every day, even when you don't use it. If you need to go away for a few days and can't feed it, keep it refrigerated.

# Sourdough loaf with spices

This is a classic Danish white bread that we eat regularly for lunch. *Makes 1 large loaf*

>   150g (5½oz) biga (see left)
>   400ml (1¾ cups) buttermilk
>   600–700g (4¼–5 cups) white strong
>       (bread) flour
>   2 tbsp caraway seeds
>   1 tbsp coriander seeds, lightly crushed
>   8g (2 tsp) sea salt flakes

Mix the biga and buttermilk together, then add the flour, spices and salt and stir well for about 5 minutes. Let the dough rest for 10 minutes, then stir again. Cover the bowl with a towel and leave the dough to rise for about 2 hours. Tip it into a a large loaf tin, about 30 x 10cm (12 x 4in) and 10cm (4in) deep, and let it rise again for 1 hour.

Preheat the oven to fan 180°C/400°F/gas 6.

Brush the top of the loaf with water, and bake it for 45 minutes. Remove it from the loaf tin and let it cool on a wire rack.

**143**

# Eggs

I always buy organic eggs, often from a small shop in Copenhagen that gets them directly from a small Danish egg farm. They come in beautiful colours, the yolk is as yellow as the sun, and they are very tasty.

## Hard-boiled eggs

There are endless ways to boil an egg and most families swear by one way or another. This is mine. Place the eggs in a small saucepan and pour cold water over, so they are covered. Bring to the boil and then let them boil for 4 minutes. Take the saucepan off the heat, pour out the boiling water and pour plenty of cold water over the eggs. After 10 minutes, peel them; they are ready to be used.

## Poached eggs

Crack 1 egg open and tip it into a small cup. Add a dash of white wine vinegar to a pan of steadily simmering water and create a whirlpool in the water using a whisk. Slowly tip the egg into the whirlpool, white first. Cook for 2–3 minutes, then remove with a slotted spoon and place the poached egg on kitchen paper to drain off excess water. Now poach the remaining eggs, one at a time.

# Mayonnaise

This is one of the most basic ingredients you can use when making *smørrebrød*, but one that can be tweaked almost infinitely to your liking. The benefit of a home-made mayonnaise is that the flavour is clean. Most bought mayonnaise tastes too much of sugar and vinegar, which then become the dominating flavour in the *smørrebrød*.

# Classic mayonnaise

*Makes 300ml (1¼ cups), or enough for 20 servings*

> 2 organic egg yolks
> 1 tbsp Dijon mustard
> 1 tsp white wine vinegar
> 250ml (1 cup) flavourless cold-pressed oil
> sea salt flakes and freshly ground black pepper

Whisk the egg yolks in a bowl, then add the mustard and vinegar and whisk together for 5 minutes. I prefer to use a food processor or electric hand whisk for this.

Gradually add about half the oil, very slowly at first, whisking continuously, until thickened and emulsified. Continue adding the remaining oil gradually, whisking continuously. Season with a pinch each of salt and pepper. Store in a sterilized jar (see page 164) in the fridge for up to 1 week.

**Opposite,**
**from top:**
Chilli, Classic,
Aubergine, Lemon,
and Tarragon
mayonnaise

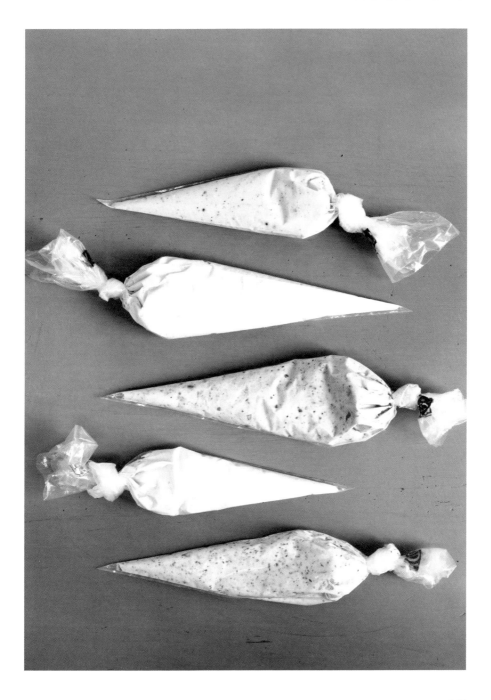

## Aubergine mayonnaise

*Makes 300ml (1¼ cups), or enough for 20 servings*

2 aubergines (eggplant)
2 tbsp olive oil
sea salt flakes and lots of freshly
   ground pepper
2 organic egg yolks
1 tbsp Dijon mustard
1 tbsp lemon juice
1 tbsp white wine vinegar
250ml (1 cup) flavourless
   cold-pressed oil

Preheat the oven to fan 180°C/400°F/gas 6. Cut the aubergines into medium-sized cubes, skin on, and mix with the olive oil and some salt and pepper. Bake them for 20 minutes, then leave to cool.

   Make the mayonnaise as for Classic mayonnaise (see page 146), then whisk in the baked aubergines. Store as for Classic mayonnaise.

## Tarragon mayonnaise

*Makes 300ml (1¼ cups), or enough for 20 servings*

2 organic egg yolks
1 tbsp Dijon mustard
2 tbsp tarragon leaves, finely chopped
1 tsp tarragon white wine vinegar
250ml (1 cup) flavourless
   cold-pressed oil
sea salt flakes and freshly
   ground pepper

Make the mayonnaise as for Classic mayonnaise (see page 146), whisking in the tarragon and vinegar with the mustard. Store as for Classic mayonnaise.

# Lemon mayonnaise

*Makes 300ml (1¼ cups), or enough for 20 servings*

2 organic egg yolks
1 tbsp Dijon mustard
2 tbsp lemon juice
2 tbsp finely grated unwaxed
    lemon zest
250ml (1 cup) flavourless
    cold-pressed oil
sea salt flakes and freshly
    ground black pepper

Make the mayonnaise as for Classic mayonnaise (see page 146), whisking in the lemon juice and zest with the mustard. Store as for Classic mayonnaise.

# Chilli mayonnaise

*Makes 300ml (1¼ cups), or enough for 20 servings*

2 organic egg yolks
1 tbsp Dijon mustard
1 tbsp lime juice
1 tbsp chilli flakes
250ml (1 cup) flavourless
    cold-pressed oil
sea salt flakes and lots freshly
    ground pepper

Make the mayonnaise as for Classic mayonnaise (see page 146), whisking in the lime juice and chilli flakes with the mustard. Store as for Classic mayonnaise.

# Quick-cured salmon

This is not gravadlax, which is cured for three days, but a quicker
– though no less delicious – version. *Makes 600g (1lb 5oz)*

> 600g (1lb 5oz) salmon fillet, skin on
> 30g (2½ tsp) granulated sugar
> 50g (¼ cup) coarse sea salt
> ½ tbsp dill seeds, coarsely crushed
> ½ tbsp fennel seeds, coarsely crushed
> ½ tbsp coarsely ground black pepper
> 1 tbsp coriander seeds, coarsely crushed

Line a ceramic dish at least 40cm (15in) long with cling film
(plastic wrap) to overhang the sides, and place the salmon fillet
skin-side down in the dish. Mix all the ingredients for the cure
and spoon the mixture evenly over the salmon, making sure the
whole fillet is covered.

   Wrap the cling film up tightly around the fillet so the mixture
stays in place. Refrigerate for 1 day or overnight. The next day,
it is ready to use.

   The salmon will keep in the refrigerator for 2–3 days.

# Liver pâté

Another family recipe from my grandmother. I have tried many versions, but for me this is the best. *Fills a 1-litre (34fl oz) mould*

5–6 small canned anchovy fillets
40g (3 tbsp) salted butter, plus more for the mould
40g (5 tbsp) plain (all-purpose) flour
450ml (1¾ cups) semi-skimmed milk
1 large onion, grated
3 tsp sea salt flakes
1½ tsp freshly ground black pepper
¼ tsp freshly grated nutmeg
1 tsp ground allspice
225g (8oz) minced (ground) pork back fat, or flare
500g (1lb 2oz) minced pig's liver
2 small eggs, lightly beaten
2–3 slices of smoked bacon
3 bay leaves

**Variation:**
Fry 150g (5½oz) sliced smoked bacon in its own fat until crispy, then remove from the pan. In the same pan, fry 200g (7oz) trimmed and sliced mushrooms in a little of the bacon fat. Serve the pâté in slices with the fried bacon and mushrooms on top.

Mash the anchovies until they become a lumpy paste. Melt the butter in a heavy pan, add the flour and mix to form a roux. Little by little add the milk, constantly stirring. Bring to the boil and add the anchovies, onion, salt, pepper, nutmeg and allspice. Add the fat to the boiling sauce, stirring until it melts. Add the liver and stir until evenly distributed. Remove the pan from the heat and cool slightly, then add the eggs and stir well.

Preheat the oven to 180°C/350°F/gas 4. Pour the pâté mixture into a 1-litre/34fl oz terrine mould that's been buttered or lined with greaseproof paper, placing the bacon slices and bay leaves on top. Put the mould in a roasting tray. Pour some hot water into the tray to come halfway up the sides of the mould. Carefully slide into the oven and bake, uncovered, for 1 hour and 15 minutes.

Remove the pâté from the oven and let cool before slicing.

# Paper-thin chocolate pieces

*Makes 300g (10½oz)*

> 300g (10½oz) dark (bittersweet) chocolate,
> 60% cocoa solids

Finely chop the chocolate and melt two-thirds of it in a
heatproof bowl suspended over simmering water (make sure
the bowl does not touch the water), or a bain-marie. When it
has melted and reached a temperature of 50°C (122°F), add the
rest of the chopped chocolate. Mix well until all the chocolate
has melted. Gently heat all the chocolate in the bain-marie until
it reaches a temperature of 31°C (88°F). Now the chocolate is
ready to use.

Spread out the melted chocolate on a piece of baking
parchment. Using a sharp knife, cut a pattern of pieces
measuring about 7 x 5cm (2¾ x 2in) through the still-melted
chocolate. Leave to cool and set before separating into pieces.

# Fig paste
*Makes 1 roll*

250g (9oz) dried figs
200g (7oz) pitted dates
2 tbsp unsweetened desiccated coconut

Cut each fig into 4, place in a bowl and pour over boiling water
to cover. Leave to rest for 30 minutes, then drain well. Put the
figs and dates in a food processor and blend into an even paste.

Form the paste into a sausage about 5cm (2in) in diameter.
Put the coconut on a plate, roll the fig paste log in this, then
wrap tightly in baking parchment and leave to rest in the
fridge overnight.

Cut the paste into slices to top your open sandwiches.

# Crispy onions

*Makes enough for 10–12 smørrebrød*

750g (1lb 10oz) onions, finely sliced
50g (6 tbsp) plain (all-purpose) flour
1 tbsp sea salt flakes, plus more
   to taste
1 litre (4¼ cups) flavourless vegetable
   oil, for deep-frying

Place the sliced onions in a bowl with the flour and salt and mix very well, until the onions are covered with flour. Pour them into a sieve to get rid of any extra flour.

Heat the oil in a frying pan. Make sure the oil is hot by dropping in a slice of onion; if its sizzles, it is ready. Reduce the heat a little and add one-third of the sliced onions. Be careful – it may spit! Don't leave; instead, stir occasionally. Fry until light brown and crispy.

Using a skimmer, transfer the onions to a plate lined with kitchen paper and sprinkle with a little more salt. Repeat the process with the other batches.

# Pesto

If you can't get lovage, just use the same amount of parsley instead. *Makes about 300ml (1¼ cups), or enough for 20 servings*

50g (1¾oz) curly parsley,
   stalks and leaves
50g (1¾oz) lovage, stalks and leaves
50g (⅓ cup) blanched almonds
1 garlic clove
1 tbsp salted capers
150ml (⅔ cup) extra virgin olive oil,
   plus more to seal
2 tbsp lemon juice
sea salt flakes and freshly ground
   black pepper

Blend all the ingredients in a food processor to a smooth paste, seasoning to taste with salt and pepper.

Use the pesto immediately, or pack it into a clean jar, making sure there are no air bubbles, and seal the surface with oil, before screwing on the lid. The pesto will keep for 1 week, as long as it is always covered with a seal of oil.

# Rhubarb compote

*Serves 6–8*

1kg (2lb 4oz) rhubarb
juice of ½ lemon
300g (1½ cups) caster (granulated)
    sugar, plus more to taste
1 tsp sea salt flakes
1 small onion, finely chopped
30g (1oz) root ginger, peeled
    and finely chopped
1 small red chilli, deseeded and
    finely chopped
seeds from 5 cardamom pods

Trim and rinse the rhubarb stalks, then cut them into 2cm (¾in) pieces. Mix them with all the other ingredients in a saucepan, then bring to the boil over a medium heat. Let simmer gently until the sugar has dissolved and the rhubarb is almost tender, about 10 minutes. Season to taste with sugar.

Remove the rhubarb from the liquid using a slotted spoon. Let cool before serving. This will keep in the fridge for a few days.

# Shaken redcurrants

*Serves 4*

300g (3 cups) redcurrants
200g (1 cup) caster (granulated)
    sugar

Rinse the redcurrants in cold water and drain well. Spread them out on a large tray and sprinkle with the sugar. Shake the tray, and then leave until the sugar has dissolved, shaking the tray occasionally.

# Asier (classic Danish pickles)

Try to grow dill flowers of your own; it is very simple. Pick them in late summer and hang them upside down in a dark place until they are dry. They give an excellent taste to all sorts of pickled vegetables. Asier belongs to the cucumber family and you only find it for sale in Denmark and Germany, where it is also common to grow it in your garden. A great friend of mine living in London decided, after having tasted my pickled asier, that she could not live without them. So now she grows asier on her roof terrace, just so she can make her own Danish pickles. *Makes 2 x 1-litre (34fl oz) jars*

2kg (4lb 8oz) asier, or replace with marrow, if necessary
50–75g (¼–⅓ cup) sea salt flakes
1 dill flower, divided into 4

### for the brine
1.5 litres (6½ cups) apple cider vinegar
750g (3¾ cups) granulated sugar
2 tbsp yellow mustard seeds
1 tbsp black peppercorns

Peel the asiers (or marrows), cut them in half lengthways and scrape out the seeds. Cut them into 1cm (½in) slices. Sprinkle with the salt, cover with a clean towel and set aside in a cool place for 2–3 hours.

Rinse the salted asier slices in cold water and wipe them lightly with a clean tea towel. Place the slices in 4 sterilized 500-ml (18fl oz) jars (see page 164) and top each with a section of dill flower.

Bring all the ingredients for the brine to the boil in a pan, whisking until the sugar has dissolved. Pour the hot brine over the asier in the jars and immediately seal. Leave for 3 weeks before eating.

**Opposite, from left:**
Pickled gherkins, Pickled beetroot (see page 162), and Asier

# Pickled gherkins

*Makes 2 x 1-litre (34fl oz) jars*

2kg (4lb 8oz) small pickling
cucumbers

### for the brine

200g (7oz) salt
1 litre (4¼ cups) apple cider vinegar
400g (2 cups) caster (granulated)
    sugar
1 bunch of dill, chopped
2 tsp black peppercorns
2 tsp yellow mustard seeds,
7–8cm (3in) piece of fresh
    horseradish, peeled and sliced

For the brine, pour 1 litre (4¼ cups) water
into a saucepan and add the salt. Bring to
the boil, then let it cool down. Rinse the
cucumbers carefully and prick each one
5–6 times with a fork. Place the cucumbers
in a bowl and cover them with the cold
brine, keeping them down with a plate.
Set them aside in a cold place overnight.

The next day, drain the cucumbers and
wipe with kitchen paper. Bring the vinegar,
400ml (1⅔ cups) water and the sugar to
the boil and let it boil for a few minutes.

Divide the cucumbers, dill, peppercorns,
mustard seeds and horseradish among
sterilized jars (see page 164). Cover with
the boiling vinegar and seal the jars. Stored
in a cold place, they keep for 6 months.

# Pickled beetroot

*Makes a 1-litre (34fl oz) jar*

1 kg (2lb 4oz) small beetroot
sea salt flakes

### for the brine

750ml (3¼ cups) apple cider vinegar
400g (2 cups) granulated sugar
1 tbsp black peppercorns
1 tbsp coriander seeds
1 cinnamon stick
2 bay leaves

Peel the beetroot and boil them in salted
water for 15 minutes, checking after
10 minutes; they need to retain some bite.

For the brine, bring all the ingredients
to the boil in a saucepan, whisking until
the sugar has dissolved. Take off the heat
and cool.

Drain the cooked beetroot, then pour
a lot of cold water over them. When cool
enough to handle, rub off the peel with
your fingers. Cut the beetroot into wedges.
Pack them in sterilized jars (see page 164),
pressing them together, then cover with
brine and seal immediately. Leave for
3 weeks before eating.

# Sweet and sour cucumber

*Makes enough for 4–6 pieces of smørrebrød*

2 large cucumbers

### for the brine
250ml (1 cup) distilled (clear)
vinegar (5% acidity)
125g (⅔ cup) caster (granulated)
sugar
pinch of sea salt flakes and freshly
ground black pepper

Whisk the vinegar with 50ml (3½ tbsp)
water, sugar, salt and pepper until the sugar
has completely dissolved.

Cut the cucumber into thin slices. If you
have a mandolin, use that, otherwise use
a very sharp knife. Place the cucumber in
the vinegar. Leave to rest for at least 1 hour,
folding gently now and then.

When ready to serve the cucumber, take
it out of the vinegar with a slotted spoon.
The vinegar brine can be reused again and
again for weeks.

# Horseradish cream

*Makes 250g (1 cup)*

100g (⅓ cup) Greek yogurt
100g (⅓ cup) full-fat crème fraîche
30g (1oz) freshly grated horseradish
1–2 tbsp lime juice
1 tsp caster (granulated) sugar
sea salt flakes and freshly ground
black pepper

Mix the yogurt and crème fraîche together
gently, then mix in the grated horseradish.
Add the lime juice and sugar and gently mix
again. Season to taste with salt and pepper.

# Mustard pickles

The best pickles I know of; this is my mother's recipe. I use the pickles in the Rémoulade (here on this page), but also to serve just as pickles for meat, fried fish or fishcakes. *Makes about 400g (14oz)*

> 750g (1lb 10oz) green tomatoes, cut into chunks
> 1kg (2lb 4oz) courgettes (zucchini), cut into chunks
> 350g (12oz) onions, cut into chunks
> 35g (3 tbsp) sea salt flakes, or to taste
> 500ml (2 cups) apple cider vinegar
> 50ml (3 tbsp) lemon juice
> 400g (2 cups) caster (granulated) sugar, or to taste
> 40g (¼ cup) plain (all-purpose) flour
> 2½ tbsp mustard seeds, ground
> 2–3 tbsp curry powder, or to taste

Blend the tomatoes, courgettes and onions until very fine in a blender or food processor, or with a hand blender. Mix with the salt, then set aside for 3–4 hours in a cool place.

Pour the vegetables into a jelly bag and leave to drain for a couple of hours. Then place the vegetables in a big saucepan with 400ml (1⅔ cups) water and 75ml (5 tbsp) of the vinegar. Bring to the boil while stirring, then let it simmer over a very low heat for 20 minutes. Once more, pour the vegetables into a jelly bag and leave to drain for some hours – even better overnight – until rather dry.

Place the vegetable mixture in a big saucepan, then add the remaining vinegar and the lemon juice. Mix the remaining ingredients in a bowl, then stir into the vegetables. Bring to the boil, still stirring, then let it simmer for 30 minutes over a very low heat, stirring often. Season to taste with more salt, curry powder and sugar. Pour the pickles into sterilized jars (see below) and seal them. Stored in a cold place, they will keep for 1 year.

To sterilize jars, stand the clean jars upright with their lids in a large pot or saucepan and fill with water to cover the jars. Bring the water to the boil and boil for 5 minutes. Carefully remove the jars and stand them upside-down on a clean tea towel to drain. Set them the right way up again, fill and seal while still warm.

# Rémoulade

*Makes about 400g (14oz)*

> 200g (7oz) Mustard pickles (on this page)
> 150g (5½oz) Classic mayonnaise (see page 146)
> 50g (3 tbsp) full-fat natural yogurt
> sea salt flakes and freshly ground black pepper

Drain the pickles a little in a sieve if you do not want the rémoulade to be too runny. Then mix them in a bowl with the mayonnaise and yogurt. Season to taste with salt and pepper.

# Roasted pork

*Serves 6*

1kg (2lb 4oz) pork loin on the bone,
    skin-on, rind scored
sea salt flakes and freshly ground
    black pepper
2 bay leaves
5 cloves

Preheat the oven to fan 200°C/425°F/gas 7.
    Make sure the pork skin is scored well,
meaning that it has been cut through the
skin down to the fat. Rub salt and pepper
into the cuts in the skin, and tuck in the bay
leaves and cloves.

    Place the pork in a roasting tray and
roast for 1 hour and 15 minutes. The inside
temperature should be 58°C (136°F). If it
isn't, then roast it a bit more. Leave to rest
before carving.

# Sautéed red cabbage

*Serves 6–8*

1kg (2lb 4oz) red cabbage
50g (3½ tbsp) salted butter
1 onion, finely chopped
4 cloves
2 bay leaves
50g (¼ cup) caster (granulated) sugar
2–3 tbsp redcurrant jelly
1 tbsp apple cider vinegar
1 tbsp duck fat
sea salt flakes and freshly ground
    black pepper

Cut the red cabbage into medium slices
– not too thin. Melt the butter in a big
saucepan and sauté the cabbage, turning
it often, until shiny. Add all the remaining
ingredients, except the salt and pepper,
together with 50ml (3½ tbsp) water.
Cover with a lid and let it simmer for
2 hours. Finally, season generously to
taste with salt and pepper.

# Frikadeller (meatballs)

*Makes about 18*

250g (7oz) minced (ground) beef
250g (7oz) minced (ground) pork
1 onion, finely chopped
2 tbsp thyme leaves
2 eggs, lightly beaten
3 tbsp breadcrumbs
2 tbsp plain (all-purpose) flour
100ml (⅓ cup) whole milk
1–2 tsp sea salt flakes and freshly
    ground black pepper
1–2 tbsp extra virgin olive oil
2–3 tbsp butter

Mix the meat, onion, thyme and eggs
together and beat well. Stir in the
breadcrumbs and flour and beat again.
Finally, mix in the milk and season with
the salt and pepper. Preheat the oven to
fan 180°C/400°F/gas 6.
    Shape the meatball mixture into small,
round balls. Heat the olive oil and butter in
a large frying pan and fry the meatballs on
all sides until golden brown. Transfer to an
ovenproof dish and bake for 10 minutes.

# Rullepølse (rolled pork)

This is a Danish classic that can be made with pork, lamb or veal. It's made over a few days, then you can cut it into smaller pieces and freeze it. This is my grandmother's recipe. *Serves 4*

### for the brine
150g (5½oz) salt
75g (6 tbsp) caster (granulated) sugar
2 bay leaves
small bunch of thyme
1 tbsp black peppercorns
5 cloves
1 onion, halved

### for the rullepølse
1 whole boned pork belly
50g (¼ cup) coarse sea salt
20g (3 tbsp) freshly ground black pepper
5g (1½ tsp) ground allspice
6 gelatine leaves

Place all the ingredients for the brine in a saucepan with 1 litre (4¼ cups) water and bring to the boil, stirring to dissolve the sugar and salt. Leave to cool.

Trim the meat, removing most of the fat. Sprinkle with the salt and spices. Soak the gelatine leaves in cold water for 5–10 minutes, then squeeze out the excess water, and place the leaves on the flesh side of the meat to cover. Roll the meat very tightly lengthways, fat side out, then tie it with kitchen string at 2.5cm (1in) intervals. Place the meat in the cold brine and leave for 48 hours in a cool place.

Put the *Rullepølse* in a saucepan, cover with fresh water and bring to the boil. Let it simmer for about 1 hour. It is ready when it feels tender when pierced with a carving fork. Remove from the saucepan and, while it's still warm, place it in a loaf tin. Put another loaf tin on top and weight it down with something heavy, to press. Chill for 24 hours. Slice thinly to serve.

# A note on herbs

Though it is deceptively simple, there is a real art to making truly great *smørrebrød*. Fresh herbs are an essential part of that art, both for the flavour possibilities they bring to the table, and for their decorative nature. These are the herbs I use the most. Some are not available in supermarkets, but all are very easy (and cheap) to grow. The best herb seeds can be bought online.

### Chervil
The very slight aniseed tang of this clean-tasting leaf goes well with egg, tomato, potato, beef, salt beef and pork.

### Chives
These oniony strands are great with egg, tomato, potato, beef or salt beef and *Rullepølse* (see page 171).

### Coriander (cilantro)
A good partner to avocado, tomato, potato, prawns, cod and beef.

### Cress
I think this goes well on most *smørrebrød*, and is traditionally used with egg, potato, beef tartare or roast or salt beef, and salami.

### Dill
A perfect partner to all seafood (and particularly well known with salmon), dill is also marvellous with chicken, salt beef and horseradish, and potato.

### Edible flowers, such as violets
Scatter these on *smørrebrød* with cheese, banana, or peach.

### Lovage
A celery note makes lovage lovely with potato, cod, beef, chicken, egg and tomato, processed into pesto, or used to flavour mayonnaise.

### Parsley, curly
This goes well with salt beef, *Rullepølse* (see page 171), egg, tomato, potato and chicken.

### Parsley, flat-leaf
This variety goes well with any meat, but is especially lovely in chicken salad and bashed into pesto.

### Sorrel
The slight citrus tang of this herb is very good with cheese or fish.

### Tarragon
With chicken or potatoes, this is a match made in heaven, but it is also good with prawns, beef and horseradish. And, of course, in mayonnaise (see page 148).

# index

# acknowledgments

I'd like to thank my family for their never-failing support and love. A special thank you to my mother for sharing recipes with me. I'd like to thank my amazing assistant, Anne Sofie Rørth, who really knows what it takes to make a cookbook. To Thomas Møller and Stig Jensen for help with the cooking and ideas. To the whole team at Hahnemanns Køkken. 1000 TAK Columbus Leth – working with you is fun and easy.

Thanks to the best agent, Heather Holden-Brown, for support and good advice. To Sarah Lavelle for continuing to believe in me. To Céline Hughes for her patience and being true to my ideas and writing. To Helen Lewis for 10 great years – I will miss you. To Katherine Keeble for a clean and beautiful layout. To Margaux Durigon and Becky Smedley for working hard to sell and promote my books. And 1000 TAK to the rest of the team at Quadrille.